Inside King Kong

Inside King Kong

A journal

Will Shephard

CHAPLIN BOOKS
www.chaplinbooks.co.uk

First published in 2014 by Chaplin Books
This edition published in 2021

Copyright © 2014, 2021 Will Shephard
ISBN: 978-1-909183-56-8

The moral right of Will Shephard to be identified as the author of this work has been asserted in accordance with the Copyright, Designs and Patents Act of 1988.

All rights reserved. No part of this publication may be reproduced, stored in any retrieval system or transmitted in any form or by any means, electronic, mechanical, photocopying, recording or otherwise, without the prior written permission of the copyright holder for which application should be addressed in the first instance to the publishers. No liability shall be attached to the author, the copyright holder or the publishers for loss or damage of any nature suffered as a result of the reliance on the reproduction of any of the contents of this publication or any errors or omissions in the contents.

All photographs were taken by Will Shephard and are the copyright of Will Shephard Works LLC; pictures of Will himself were kindly taken by colleagues on the set, and were either taken with his camera or given to him without claim to ownership, limitation or restriction on use or reproduction.

A CIP catalogue record for this book is available from The British Library

Design by Michael Walsh at The Better Book Company
Additional typography and layout by Andrews UK Limited
www.andrewsuk.com

Chaplin Books
5 Carlton Way
Gosport PO12 1LN
Tel: 023 9252 9020
www.chaplinbooks.co.uk

PROLOGUE

I still fail to understand how I wandered into my present circumstances. My fellow teachers at the small college where I'd been working were baffled by my decision to quit and cast myself headlong into the ranks of the unemployed. Why had I done it? To become one of the legion of hopefuls who follow the lure of wealth and fame, hoping to sell their faces, bodies, and perhaps even their souls in the gabbling marketplace of the entertainment industry. After all, this is Hollywood!

But months have gone by. Copies of my photograph and resumé are now lining the wastebaskets of dozens of agents and casting directors. On many a hazy afternoon, with the orange sun hanging motionless in the sky, I just walk the streets, wondering what prompted me to abandon myself to this self-defeating folly. Today my legs ache with fatigue and as I sit on a hard wooden bench at a bus-stop on Hollywood Boulevard, I doze off for a few minutes. There is no bus in sight.

Not even a second seems to elapse before I find myself standing on an enormous plain stretching to tall blue mountains on the horizon. I have the unmistakable feeling that something is stalking me, and I am desperately looking for a place to hide. There are no trees or any sort of cover – only small, straggly bushes growing out of hard, inhospitable ground. I lie down beneath one of these bushes and try to become completely immobile in the hope of avoiding detection. Soon I become aware of a gigantic presence. Its footsteps shake the earth and its gargantuan form casts such a large shadow that it seems to darken the entire plain. It's moving towards me. I hold my breath. The thunderous footsteps approach, then stop and seem to pause directly above the feeble bush under which I am trying to hide. My heart freezes. I daren't look up into the face of my pursuer. Suddenly the gigantic figure moves away, across the plain to the mountains, where it mercifully vanishes. I have been spared for the moment, but I am sure the monster saw me and is only biding its time before it returns.

I awake with a start as the huge tires of the bus screech to a halt inches in front of my feet. How many times in our dreams do we fall, and from what perilous heights, only to avert the terror of our doom by opening our eyes to fix our gaze on familiar objects – a lamp, a mirror, or picture on the wall – and find rescue. Oh, I am a strong dreamer; believe me. I have traveled through time and watched bubbles rising from the ooze of a prehistoric lagoon – silver bubbles, shimmering and dancing upwards in the black-green water, breaking the surface and revealing a pair of glassy reptilian eyes, unseen for over a million years.

The bus door closes and the smoking beast draws away, leaving a lingering cloud of noxious exhaust.

Perhaps I have always had a dangerous tendency to abandon the tediousness of 'reality' in favor of the glorious phantasmagoria of imaginative voyaging, but since I ventured out into in the harsh world beyond the protective walls of academia, I've been doing this more often. After all, I've had plenty of time on my hands. Wherever I have looked for work – in shops, bookstores or health clubs – I have been rejected and always for the same reason – I am 'overqualified and under-skilled'. I did finally get a job, though, as a driver for the Beverly Hills Cab Company and I'm succeeding in supporting myself on the grime of the steering wheel and my passengers' fares. I have also attracted the attention of an agent who represents a variety of clients, including animals, children, variety artists and actors, from a windowless office in a collection of commercial warehouses near Santa Monica Boulevard and Labrea. Heartened by my apparent change of fortune, I engaged an answering service for the privilege of calling in twice a day to learn that I am 'clear', an obvious euphemism for not being wanted. But then everything changes: I get a call from my agent that looks like it will set in motion one of the greatest fantasies of all time.

Tuesday July 22, 1975

"Can you be at the offices of Dino De Laurentiis in Beverly Hills by 10.00am?"

"Of course – sure! What's it all about?"

"They're looking for people who can do animal movements – that's all I know. No, wait a minute – it says here they want people who can do apes."

Apes? There was a recent movie about space voyagers who return to earth to find it dominated by a species of highly developed apes. Improbable though it seems, it was a box-office smash, something that is referred to in the trade publications as either 'Boffo', 'Socko-Boffo' or 'Boffola', depending upon the degree of financial success. The ape movie was definitely 'Boffola' so maybe I'm being interviewed for a sequel. Donning a green jogging suit and sneakers to give myself an athletic appearance, I make my way towards Beverly Hills. I am well aware that Mr De Laurentiis is one of the most powerful, prolific and influential producers in the global film industry, and it is not without a certain amount of awe that I enter his plush offices at 202 North Canon Drive.

As I enter the vestibule of the two-storey building, I am immediately impressed by the spiral staircase that leads to the upper floor. Several portraits of international film stars line the walls, and the receptionist sits at a modern-styled shape that I take to be a desk. She is busy pushing buttons in an elaborate phone console with lines apparently connected to Rome, Paris, London and New York. As I approach her, I notice that she is an attractive example of the *mode du jour* – neither solely feminine nor masculine in her dress, she presents a charming portrait of casual attire popular in Beverly Hills: short hair, bellbottom jeans, and a short-sleeved madras print shirt left unbuttoned in the front just far enough to give a stimulating preview of her beguiling bosom.

"Can I help you?" she asks.

"Yes, I've come to see someone named 'Federico' about a De Laurentiis picture."

"Just take a seat – someone will help you in a moment."

She smiles, exuding subtle enticements of the most pleasant nature – a hint of the exotic yet modestly contained, in keeping with her employer's respectability. It seems that female receptionists the world over are chosen for their ability to charm and elicit cooperation and in this case, I am compelled to do anything she asks me. The shining countenances of the stars photos hanging on the walls seem to nod in agreement and give an almost aristocratic aspect to the surrounding offices.

Perhaps only a moment passes before I am ushered down a hall and into a spacious office for my meeting with the mysterious Federico. I scrutinize everyone I see, hoping to detect the face and figure of my prospective employer, but receive no answer to the question in my gaze. Strange, there is no last name – only 'Federico'. Perhaps he is a lower-level functionary, someone who has the odious task of weeding out the grossly ill-suited whose agents have submitted them, willy-nilly, for a particular part.

There is a slight commotion in the hallway, then a young man enters the office with a bunch of animal photographs under his arm. Long, dark hair falls to his shoulders and frames an attractive face. His eyes are dark brown, and a confident smile gives his features an amused expression. He is slim and his white shirt and trousers form a contrast to his olive complexion. We stand eye-to-eye, of medium stature on the shortish side, and I take an instant liking to him. He doesn't volunteer what his precise function is in the De Laurentiis organization. He speaks with a slight accent, and I guess he is Italian.

I introduce myself, and hand him my 8 x 10 glossy photos and my resumé.

Surely this shot of me as Jack London will show the mysterious Federico that I'm a real actor?

"My agent told me on the phone that you were looking for actors who could do animal movements, but she didn't tell me what the film was about," I say.

"It's-a King Kong," Federico says.

"You mean a remake of the 1933 film?" I stammer.

"Yes."

"What's the role I'm being considered for?"

"It's-a Kong."

Needless to say, I am floored. Auditioning for the part of King Kong goes beyond anything I might have imagined. Not even knowing exactly what I am saying, I launch into my best job of salesmanship, trying to impress Federico with my qualifications for playing the role of a forty-foot tall gorilla.

"Well, the nose is not quite right, and the eyes are the wrong color," he says.

"Certainly a talented make-up artist could correct the small discrepancies."

"Well, maybe. Would you be willing to show your animal movements to the director?"

"Certainly – by all means."

"Good. We'll be in touch with you," Federico says.

We shake hands and my interview is concluded.

I leave the De Laurentiis offices in a daze. The whole idea of *playing* the role of King Kong seems utterly preposterous. It's like being asked to play the role of Moby Dick or Godzilla – no, that has already been done. My imagination reels at the implications of playing the tallest, darkest leading man (well, ape) in the history of motion pictures! The original *King Kong* made at RKO studios in 1933 is a film classic, a superb example of savage spectacle. My predecessor (I can't resist the temptation to see myself in the role already) terrified and amazed motion-picture audiences everywhere as 'The Eighth Wonder Of The World'. My father took me to see the movie when I was a child, and even the slightest suggestion that I might follow in Kong's gargantuan footsteps shakes me to the core. To see what he saw, to inhabit his fabulous lost island kingdom, to battle and conquer prehistoric monsters, to fall helplessly in love with a tiny beauty, and to die an heroic death from the top of one of the world's greatest buildings – all this is too much to contain within the bounds of idle speculation. 'Best not to think about it too much,' I tell myself.

Actors have to get used to the idea of rejection when auditioning for roles. As an unctuous theatre producer once told me as he put his arm across my shoulder, "It's all about the vicissitudes of casting, Will."

Nevertheless, as I approach the garage of the Beverly Hills Cab Company to get my cab and go to work later that night, one of my childhood dreams reaches out and stirs my memory:

I had dreamed I was a prisoner in a dungeon built in the bowels of some old castle to inflict despair in the hearts of those poor souls whose misfortune it had been to sink so low. There were only two cells in the dungeon, cells which seemed more like cages since they stood alone in the center of the cold, stone floor. In the cage next to mine stood an enormous gorilla who regarded me with all the rage it could muster in its hideous face. A jailer, holding a tray of food, descended the stone steps leading into the dungeon. He approached the gorilla's cage and offered the tray of food. The gorilla reached through the bars, placed both of its large, hairy hands on either side of the jailer's head and, giving it two or three twists, lifted the jailer's head off his shoulders. The headless jailer, thus rejected by the ungrateful beast, merely turned on his heels and walked away.

Wednesday January 14, 1976

Day after day I've been making calls to my agent, only to learn that they have not heard from the elusive Federico. I can't see myself ever getting off the cab-stand at the Beverly Hilton Hotel, and this morning I am given a traffic citation for an illegal left turn. I would dispute it, but I feel so crestfallen about Kong that I decide not to take the issue to court as I would normally do. Beverly Hills is one of the more pleasant areas to drive a cab, but I have become jaded with the lovely palm-tree-lined drives, stars' homes, and even the lively hotel trade. My evening pastry at the coffee shop of the Beverly Wilshire Hotel has lost its sugary pleasure, turning into tasteless wet cardboard in my mouth.

This morning, however, the phone in my apartment rings, and I hear the barking of an unfamiliar voice on the other end of the line.

"Shephard? This is Jack Grossberg, King Kong Productions, and I've been told to get in touch with you about the role of King Kong. Are you interested?"

"Well, yes – you see, I was expecting to hear from Federico ..."

"I'm handling this," interrupts Mr Grossberg.

"Oh, I see. Have you contacted my agent?"

"No agents! Either we talk to you or the deal's off."

"Well, in that case ..."

"Can you be over here at MGM by noon?"

"Yes – yes I think I can."

"Fine."

There is a click on the other end of the line followed by a dial tone.

I go out to my car, a small, blue Austin American given to me by my parents, who are at a loss to understand my recent career change but always encourage my ambitions. Passing a nearby tree, I brush a few pieces of rotten fruit off the hood of my car, squeeze the car out of its narrow parking space, and drive toward Culver City where the MGM studios are located. From my cab-driving experience, I vaguely remember that MGM is near a funeral parlor on Washington Boulevard. When I finally arrive at the front gate, a balding, mustachioed guard scowls at me as my car comes to a halt beside his station. I am told to park at a nearby curb and walk into the studio.

A poster of a huge gorilla decorates a door just inside the main gate. Printed in large black letters on the lintel above the door is 'KING KONG PRODUCTIONS'. A cool, blond secretary presides over the suite of offices inside.

"I've come to see Mr Grossberg about the role of King Kong," I proudly volunteer.

"Oh, you must be one of the technical consultants," she says.

"No, I don't believe so – you see, I'm an actor."

"It's all the same thing. The guys in the ape suit are referred to as 'technical consultants'. Just wait over there. "

The 'guys in the ape suit'? I manage to nod politely and sit down on one of the large leather couches. I then overhear the secretary making dinner reservations at an expensive restaurant.

"Hello, yes, I'd like to make reservations for a party of four this evening. The name is Federico De Laurentiis."

Like a clap of thunder the realization comes to me: the mysterious Federico is none other than the son of the powerful Dino. I remember now – I did see his name on a King Kong poster where he was listed as Executive Producer, but I hadn't put it together because the Federico I met only looked to be about 21 years old. I guess if your father runs the studio, you're going to be groomed from an early age to take it over someday. This would explain his manner when we met: he could afford to be direct and personable. He'd also given the impression of an amused detachment from it all, something you can do if you're not relying on the salary to survive. No wonder I'd found him so charming compared to the usual hard-nosed, avaricious, two-faced, double-dealing shysters who preside over the financial life and death of hapless artists.

A tall, stoop-shouldered man comes into the office and says, "'Lo, Mr Shephard, I'm Jack Grossberg." We shake hands, and he motions me to a chair in front of his desk. As he sits down, he takes out a pocket-sized tape recorder, lays it on the desk in front of me and turns it on.

"I'm prepared to offer you the role of King Kong if we can come to some agreement satisfactory to the producers," he says.

'Will I be the only actor doing the role?"

"No, you'll be doing it with Rick Baker. He's working on the suit and playing Kong as well. Are you interested in the role or not?"

"Interested? Yes, of course, but I ..."

"Look, Will, we've just met. Let's not start off on the wrong foot by getting into an argument. You're gonna love it here. It's a long paying job and a nice buncha people to work with."

"I'd like a Screen Actors Guild contract, because I'm a member," I say.

"Fine. We'll pay the weekly minimum. Now I'll introduce you to Rick Baker, and if you two can get along, we've made a deal."

Jack Grossberg excuses himself, having urgent business elsewhere, instructing the secretary to ask Rick Baker to come up to the office and meet me. I sink into a long, beige couch, still reeling from the speed and the matter-of-fact simplicity of our negotiation. I am happy to have secured a SAG contract – 'technical consultant' or not – because there are numerous union rules about working conditions and residuals. While waiting, I amuse myself by examining the collection of 'Kongabilia' which have been tacked up on the office walls. In addition to several tasteless photographs of gorillas distinguished for their grotesque or comic appearance, there is a flimsy beach towel imprinted with a cheap rendering of Kong atop the Empire State Building. There are also copies of articles that have appeared in various publications, describing a legal dispute between Dino De Laurentiis and Universal Pictures over the rights to the former screen classic.

Perhaps twenty minutes pass before a casually dressed young man of about my age enters the office, speaks briefly to the secretary, then seats himself beside me on the couch. He wears faded jeans, a denim shirt jacket, and discolored yellow tennis shoes. His hair is short and brown, and there is something vaguely familiar about his overall appearance. We sit together in silence for several minutes like two transients in a bus station. All at once I see what is so familiar about him. He cuts his own hair; I am sure of it! I, too, have eschewed the barber's chair for several years, entrusting my appearance to my own skill with comb and scissors in front of a bathroom mirror. And yes, there is the same evidence – the hacked uneven layers of hair in the back. Somehow, without the slightest doubt in my mind, I know he is the very person I am supposed to meet.

"Are you Rick Baker?" I ask.

"Yes," he replies, surprised by my question.

"Hello, my name is Will Shephard."

"Oh, so you're the one I was supposed to come up here and meet?"

I give the secretary an incredulous look, but she is off in the clouds somewhere between lunch and the magazine she is thumbing through.

"Well," says Rick, "why don't I show you around the plant, and we'll see if you can fit into one of the gorilla suits."

Rick directs me through a maze of bungalows towards the make-up lab, our first stop. We walk down a narrow alley between two buildings and climb a flight of stairs into a small room that is filled with plaster molds and sculptors' tools. The smell of the damp clay triggers an association, a memory from my childhood.

Between 1950 and 1952, my family lived in the Pacific Palisades and the two years we lived there stand out in my memory because of some strange fantasies I began to have at the time. One foggy day, I remember an interminable car trip with my parents and sister to visit a chinaware factory in San Pedro. I remember little about the trip except for the dusty factory and its damp smell of clay. The design on the dishes my mother bought, however, stands out in my memory. They were plain white china with a green bamboo motif. Looking at a plate, I remember feeling I was being pulled into the design. *For just a brief instant, in no more time than it takes to blink, I felt the damp mist of a jungle on my back and shoulders, and I remembered the omnipresent verdure of a tropical climate I had never seen.*

There, in front of me, resting on a workman's table, is a bust of the embryonic Kong, modeled in clay. The face and head are distinctly gorilla-like in character. The original Kong, as I recall, was a small model of an ape-like creature with the back and shoulders of a gorilla.

"You sculpted the face?" I ask Rick.

"Yes," he says, smiling with obvious pride in his work.

"It's very good."

Indeed, there are several busts of Kong around the room, each with a different expression – one angry, one proud, one puzzled, and even one smiling. The wrinkles around the wide nostrils of the nose are finely delineated, and the brow, rising toward the great crest of the head, is a wonder of line and form. As we continue our tour of the lot, I learn that Rick, a talented special-effects make-up artist, has always been interested in gorillas and in how they could be played by men in simian suits. He was the first Kong selected for the film, on the understanding that he would also help design and build the elaborate suits to be used in the picture. Presumably, the producers want an extra Kong on hand in case of emergency, and one of the reasons I have been selected is that Rick and I are about the same size.

Clay models sculpted by Rick Baker

"There were two other guys doing Kong with me before you," Rick says, "but they were too tall. The craftsmen would've had to make two versions of each miniature set for all of us to work on. Besides one of the guys didn't work out too well in the suit, and the other guy goofed around a lot. He made too many expenses-paid trips down to San Diego to look at gorillas in the zoo."

"I guess you know Federico," I say. "Can you tell me what happened to him?"

"Oh, he's still around, but Dino put Jack Grossberg in charge of production. I guess he didn't like some of the deals Federico was making."

"What do you think of Jack Grossberg?" I ask.

"He's an asshole."

"What do you mean?"

"Asshole!" Rick exclaims.

He doesn't offer to expand. For my part, I can see that Mr Grossberg is one of those studio executives who doesn't just go through the motions of carrying out his duties – namely to coerce, intimidate or otherwise control the pecking order and day-by-day operations of the production company – but does so with relish and extraordinary zeal. I'm sure there is some administrative logic to it all, but I do regret that I won't have Federico to work with instead.

Tall sound stages loom up on either side of us as we pass along the narrow roadways in between. I have never seen anything like them before, but they remind me of a valley of gigantic boulders I saw in a childhood nightmare.

In the dream, I was riding on a huge plastic fork that bounced along a string between gigantic rocks on either side of me. The rocks directly in front of me would crash together with a deafening thunder, then quickly separate. Next, the rocks behind me would crash together with the same deafening sound while my plastic fork bounced me along the string. I woke up panting with exertion.

The recollection is only momentary; it quickly vanishes in the mid-morning sun. However, a residue of my childhood dream remains, and I feel that powerful, unseen forces are at work around me.

As we walk, I reflect that a motion picture studio is an ideal environment for the fantastic, the bizarre, the breathtaking. Where else can one peer into cavernous sound stages five storeys high, each with its self-contained world? Where else can one traverse history and continents in a matter of minutes, walking from one street scene to the next? In such places the boundaries between fantasy and reality become indistinct.

It reminds me of when, one Sunday afternoon in 1962, I set out with a high-school friend to do a little exploring in San Francisco. Down by the Presidio, we noticed a cupola of some large old edifice that rose high above the surrounding houses. Upon closer inspection, we discovered it to be a huge domed rotunda. The architecture and the sculptures that decorated the sides seemed to be imitation Roman or Greek, and the structure stood in the middle of a city park, separated from the rest of the park by a large, man-made lake complete with ducks, swans, geese, popcorn bags and a few beer cans. Our curiosity was stimulated by the fact that there seemed to be no way to get to it other than across the water. We walked around the back of the structure – it roughly covered a city block – but found no entrance to the mysterious grounds, which were enclosed within impregnable walls.

Using a good measure of high-school ingenuity, we finally discovered a small hole underneath a heavy wire-mesh fence – the hole must have been made by squirrels or raccoons. With a certain amount of digging and squirming we finally managed to get underneath. We passed through a few yards of high grass and bushes and emerged to discover a fantastic lost world in the afternoon sun. The sounds of the city seemed to have disappeared, and the people in the park, across the water were obscured by tall shrubs and bushes. Huge Doric and Ionic columns, over ten feet in diameter, rose perhaps fifty or sixty feet in the air. Roman-style statues stood on pedestals high above the ground, and, here and there, a statue's fallen face gazed stonily towards the sky among thick weeds. Fragments of huge urns lay scattered about as though pushed over by an invading army, but the fragments were made out of plaster rather than stone: the whole place was a ruin. We speculated that the structure had probably been part of a World's Fair Exhibition and we later learned it was the old Palace of Fine Arts, constructed for the Panama-Pacific Exposition in 1915.

Under the immense dome, classical figures seemed to cavort across a mural whose colors remained distinct over fifty years after its creation, giving it the appearance of an extravagant movie set. And here I am, now, inside a real movie studio where such fantasies are created on a regular basis.

Thus I try to rationalise the vague uneasiness, the temporary disruption of balance I experience as I pass deeper and deeper into a world that seems both oddly familiar and completely strange. As we round a corner, approaching the Model Shop near the back of the lot, Rick explains that there are two artistic teams at work on the film – one Italian and one American – and there is a major problem with communication.

When we arrive at the Model Shop, the Italians are at lunch, and Rick seems more at ease than he might otherwise have been. The shop itself is an old corrugated metal structure with high ceilings. It obviously belongs to another era, and it is bound on two sides by small, interconnecting windows through which light enters and rests on a thin, white layer of dust that covers everything. There is something eerie about the place. This is where models, sculpted in clay, are cast in plaster molds. The plaster 'negative' is then converted to fiberglass, and the final, latex form is derived from these. Looking around, it seems the mold-makers are busy working on various shapes of miniature jungle trees. Rick and I pass into a back room that has been set aside for the Kong suits. He explains that the final suits have not been made yet, but, for the purposes of fitting, he will try one of his earlier ones on me.

He tells me to take off all my clothing except for my underwear. I step into the single-piece gorilla suit with ease, as it seems to fit me very well. The chest and abdomen are enormous, and I can't see my feet without bending over slightly. Rick explains that work in the suit is very hot and very strenuous. Wearing it, I feel a strange surge of energy, as if my imagination is already taking me to the lost world and adventures ahead.

We chat amiably on the way back to Mr Grossberg's office, and I feel that we are compatible. My feeling proves accurate for, after a brief meeting with Rick, Mr Grossberg says "Glad to have you on the team." I walk out of his office with an utter sense of amazement: I am now King Kong! I am only one of the King Kongs, of course, and more accurately, I am probably 'Second Gorilla', but I put this out of my head in favor of the incredible thought that

I have been cast in one of the greatest anonymous roles in the history of motion pictures.

As I drive home in the warm afternoon sun, some automatic pilot in my nervous system takes control of the car, and my mind becomes condensed into a drop of moisture that hurtles through time and space towards a lost world on an undiscovered island where it hovers tenuously before descending to the mist below.

As I step into the suit I feel a huge surge of energy:
I am now King Kong!

Monday February 2

Day upon day passes in blissful serenity – I am employed! The sky seems as clear as a baby's eye, the tall palms on Franklin Avenue sway to and fro in a brisk breeze, and the neighborhood cats stretch and roll on the warm pavement of the driveways. I am not needed at the studio yet, since work on the miniature sets hasn't begun. I have a pleasant amount of time to myself, and I only need to go in once a week to pick up my check.

Every day I call to see if I am needed at the studio, but I am told either that the company is preparing to leave for location in Hawaii or the gorilla suits are not ready yet. On Thursdays, when I make my routine trip to the studio, I sometimes wander down to the make-up lab or the Model Shop and stop to chat with Rick. One day I find him with his hair and face covered with flecks of white plaster. He is busy supervising the work of the mold-makers and sculptors. Here and there a model gorilla forearm reaches toward the ceiling on a wooden stand, or a hairless bust of Kong presides serenely over the dusty white prototypes of his world.

The afternoon sun filters through the high windows of the Model Shop, and a general hubbub outside the corrugated metal door announces the return of the Italians from their two-hour lunch break. They enter the shop as a group – no mean accomplishment since there are five of them. They stick together fairly closely, buttressing themselves against their American colleagues. Their collective demeanor can hardly be described as gregarious, yet, as they enter, their conversation is extremely animated. I just can't understand what they are saying. They punctuate their remarks to each other with elaborate hand gestures and active expressions with their eyebrows.

Mario Chiari, the Italian Production Designer, seems to lead this group with the poise and panache befitting his position. He wears slim, black-and-white checked trousers and a casual grey sport coat, and his grey hair and coal-black moustache give him an air of leonine respectability. He is balancing a cigarette between his thumb and forefinger. I notice that, to the European, a cigarette is a measure of personal attire that never dangles from the lower lip in the careless abandon of American smokers (unless, of course, that is the desired effect, as with Jean-Paul Belmondo). Rather it is held between the thumb and first finger or the first and middle finger as if it were meant to make a point or be used as a conductor's baton. Only the fingertips suffer slightly through this otherwise impeccable European style, by turning yellow or brown from nicotine stains.

Rick introduces me to the Italians as they pass by us, and I notice that they are all small in stature except for the translator, who is tall and thin with curly blond hair. Carlo Rambaldi, the Special Effects Designer, is a mechanical wizard who has worked for Mr De Laurentiis for many years. He is short and thin and seems to have a hunted, hyper-vigilant look about him. His hair is short and black, streaked with gray, and he has a piercing stare as if he has remained sequestered for many years, laboring over gadgets that make up the inner workings of sea serpents, cyclops, or other film monsters.

The other members of the Italian contingent, Isidoro Riponi and Paolo Seipione, are Rambaldi's assistants, and I am to become closely acquainted with them in the near future. And the near future is gradually rising out of the white dust, the clay, and the plaster all around us: this small, high ceilinged workshop is becoming the birthplace of the new King Kong. Posters and advertisements have already appeared, stating boldly that 'There is still only one King Kong'. I suppose it doesn't make any difference that there will be two of us.

Paolo Seipione and Isidoro Riponi, two of the 'Italian contingent'

As I walk back to the other end of the lot on my way to have lunch with Rick, I reflect how strangely familiar this bizarre world is to me. Film actors have always been a romantic breed to me.

I remember dining at Romanoff's Restaurant in Beverly Hills with my family one evening in 1952. I was seven years old and had no understanding of the flamboyant owner, Michael Romanoff, or the importance of this restaurant to Hollywood culture. The glitteringly elegant furnishings subdued my active imagination because I sensed I was in a very grown-up place – where nobody had any fun. My mother leaned across the table and whispered that movie stars often ate in this restaurant, and she suggested I be on the look-out for some of them. Movie stars were a mysterious, magic breed of people who adults often talked about with awe in their voices. The only movie stars I was aware of were cowboys such as Hoot Gibson, Ken Maynard and Hopalong Cassidy. Then again, there was Jane Russell who so impressed me at the age of six, in the movie *Son of Paleface*, I started wishing she were my mother. Regardless, I began to sense a greater hierarchy of movie stars beyond the realm of our miraculous television. At this, I began to look in all directions in the restaurant, hoping to see a movie star. At last, I recognized someone sitting at a table by himself. He was, in fact, a character actor, someone many people might recognize but would be unable to name. I made connection, grabbed my mother's hand and whispered loudly, "Look, Mama – there's one!" As I pointed in his direction, the character actor must have heard me, for his head seemed to sink lower into his soup, but I had him! He was my prize: I had recognized a movie star!

Friday March 19

My first day on *King Kong* has come at last! After so many fruitless calls to the production office at MGM, I am finally told to report for work on Stage 27 at 7.30am. When I arrive at the front gate, it seems that someone has forgotten to inform the guards that I really am part of the King Kong team now. This particular guard had seen me before, of course, but he refuses to recognize me. It takes some time to straighten the whole thing out.

The fact that I am fifteen minutes late on set is of no consequence whatever; I learn that a 7.30am call is, at best, hypothetical as far as actual work is concerned. The cast and crew may arrive on time, but the mobilization of all the collective energies doesn't take place until lunch. In this business, it seems, many people are being paid for just standing around. As it happens, I am not called upon to make any personal contribution today, other than my mere presence – of which everyone else seems completely unaware. The inside of the sound stage is cavernous. The top of the building rises five storeys above the concrete floor, and the semi-darkness is illuminated here and there by huge arc lamps that sputter and smoke as if on fire. I timidly help myself to a doughnut and some coffee under the glowering gaze of some of the tech crew, who don't know who I am or what I'm doing here. Clearly I am in privileged territory.

I continue to meander through a mass of electrical cables until I arrive at a miniature set that has been constructed for a test. On a large surface made up of moveable platforms strung together, a plain of miniature styrofoam boulders and rubber trees spread out in front of an enormous white screen that seems at least forty feet high and fifty feet across. I want very badly to step up onto the set and feel what it's like to be Kong, able to touch the treetops. I make no move towards the object of my fascination.

Gradually I learn the unwritten code on every motion picture: whatever the director proposes, the producer disposes, and, unless you're one of the stars or a member of their entourage, you need to keep a low profile. There is also a intricate hierarchy among the technical crews – from camera crew, to lighting, to sound – governed by the studio and the unions. In addition, there are hordes of mechanics, carpenters and electricians who move in the semi-darkness from picture to picture, rarely seeing the light of day. They are like an army of mercenaries that owe no allegiance to any particular project, though they wear windbreakers or T-shirts displaying the logo of the current production. Like all soldiers, they boast among themselves and have favorite topics of conversation: booze, women and nifty cars. They also have a curious practice of standing around in circles, producing large rolls of cash from their back pockets to wave in front of each other's noses. Apparently the one with the largest wad of cash is acknowledged top dog, unless it's a union boss who has a smaller wad, but all made up of hundred-dollar bills. The actors or stunt doubles, ironically termed 'talent' in film business lingo, are at the bottom of the pecking order unless, of course, one is a 'star.' The craft-service crew provides food and drink, including coffee and doughnuts for breaks, plus meals when required; however, no-one else is allowed to even plug in a coffee pot unless he is a member of a particular union.

Thus, the technical crews build each new film on the remains of the last, and there is no substantial difference between the rubble of last week's colossus and the beginnings of next week's extravaganza. Such a well-oiled machine moves slowly, keeping momentum in check and accumulating overtime. I quickly learn that it's best to remain invisible for as long as possible, and I am succeeding beyond my wildest dreams.

At length, I notice the Italian production crew and their tall, blond interpreter, running here and there, carrying on in a very officious manner as though their input is critical to the success of the film. There is a conspicuous absence of women on the set with one notable exception. Jessica Lange, an American model living in Paris, has been cast in the role of 'Dwan', Kong's love-interest (the role originally played by Fay Wray in the 1933 classic). This is Lange's first motion picture role, and she plays the part on the set as well. She is followed everywhere by an entourage – her hairdresser, her stand-in, her stunt double, her wardrobe mistress and a small dog that she either carries or leaves to trot along behind her.

After four hours of witnessing the buzz of activity all around me, I discover that I've been walking around in circles for quite some time. A tall fellow wearing a blue-and-white plaid shirt finally approaches me and asks if I am William Shephard. He introduces himself as Nate Haggard, one of the ADs, or Assistant Directors, on the film. By process of elimination he has accounted for everyone present with the exception of me. I ask Nate if I'm required to do anything particular. He smiles and says "No," walking away.

Suddenly, I notice Federico standing in a group of people near the center of the stage. He seems to have changed since our first meeting, not in the way he looks, but in the way he carries himself. When I first met him at the De Laurentiis offices in Beverly Hills he seemed young, of course, but he had an aura of effortless authority. Now he is wearing the Italian equivalent of a baseball cap, and he has an expensive camera hung about his neck. He smiles to those around him, but he seems somehow lacking his former poise. Now he looks like a handsome college student, home on vacation or taking a tour of the studio. I don't feel like approaching him.

Tuesday March 23

If you ever find yourself walking in a forest and come to a small pond hidden in a clearing, find a place where you can be still and remain quiet for a few minutes. Slowly, after your intrusion in the scene has been absorbed, the pond will come to life again in a mixture of sounds and movements, indicating the resumption of natural activities in its normal setting.

If, however, you expect to witness a similar phenomenon on a movie set, be prepared for disappointment. The natural state of affairs does not evolve organically as it does in, say, a bee hive or a mound of termites where independent thought is irrelevant; on the contrary, forward movement or action on a movie set only happens when unilateral agreement is reached. Ostensibly, the Director has absolute control over the workings of the production machine, but it's the Producer who holds the purse strings. Then, of course, the various unions have their say. Essentially, therefore, the activity on a movie set involves the relentless grinding down of individual resistance to the inevitable – completion of the film.

By the third day of my wanderings around Stage 27, a particular goal in the day's activities has become apparent. Although I am unfamiliar with the practice, Nate explains to me that the large white screen at the rear of the miniature artificial jungle is used for something called 'front screen projection'. A large, antique-looking apparatus that uses a tremendous amount of electricity is mounted over a camera which is focused on the miniature set in front of the screen. When the apparatus is turned on, there is a loud crack and buzz from all the electrical connections, smoke begins to billow from the top of the machine like a locomotive, and a colorful panorama seems to miraculously appear on the screen behind the set. (This is obviously a clever variation of the old rear-screen projection where actors could be filmed in front of active backgrounds like traffic, moving street scenes, and the like). The front projection technique, accomplished with mirrors, proves to be superior. Owing to the construction of the screen's reflective surface, actors can be filmed in front of the background at various distances. The scene being projected in this case is a 'plate' or piece of stock footage that has been previously shot on location. It looks amazingly real. The clouds slowly move across the sky, and the miniature set seems to blend amazingly well with the footage of the towering green peaks behind it.

Rick joins me on the set, since today one of the elaborate new Kong suits has been completed for a test. It consists of an inner suit, padded in such a way to approximate the inner musculature of the gorilla, and an outer suit of tailored bear hide. Fortunately there are no zippers. The outer suit is opened and closed with an elaborate set of invisible clasps that I learn involve a considerable amount of manipulation by the special effects crew.

The head piece is a beautifully constructed gorilla mask with wire cables attached to small mechanisms in the face that control the facial expressions. These are manually manipulated, off-camera, by a system of levers. The entire apparatus is wheeled in on a flat-bed cart by the Italians, and it looks so bizarre, a strange scene begins to form in my mind:

Tumbrels, rolling through the streets of Paris during the French Revolution; inside one is a huge gorilla wearing a frock coat and trousers. It remains stoically impassive despite the jeers and cat-calls from the mob. Abruptly, the cart comes to a halt before the guillotine, and slowly the gorilla in the frock court ascends the steps with the resolve of Sidney Carton in 'A Tale of Two

Rick Baker with one of the special effects guys

Cities'. At the top, though, the condemned gorilla breaks into a song and dance routine of 'I Went To The Animal Fair', enraging the crowd and ending with the lyric ' ... and that was the end of the monk, the monk, the monk', at which point he is forcibly shoved into place on the frame of the guillotine and the blade is dropped.

I rub my eyes and regain my composure just in time to watch Rick being put into the gorilla suit, a process I observe with a great deal of envy. Wearing only his underwear and socks, Risk steps into the inner suit with relative ease and promptly begins to perspire. Four condoms filled with water are being attached to pockets on either side of Kong's chest to give the simian breasts a certain fluidity of movement – a masterpiece of what I take to be Italian ingenuity! The outer chest is then attached, and next the arm extensions and feet are put on. Gorillas have much longer arms than humans, so the hands of Kong extend at least eight to ten inches beyond those of the man in the suit. The gorilla feet are cleverly designed, hairy, five-toed shoes that lace up at the back of the ankle. The outer suit of bear hide is then attached through a laborious system of hooks, snaps and velcro. The design, tailoring, craft and artistry is astounding.

Before putting on the suit, Rick's entire face is blackened by Bob Mills, the make-up man, with a compound of dark, powdery, diatomaceous earth that doesn't reflect light. The effect of the make-up is such that, without the Kong head, Rick has no discernible face at all until he opens his eyes and smiles. As the Kong mask is lowered over his face and attached to the rest of the costume, Rick disappears entirely. Kong's face is magnificent – proud and noble – a refreshing contrast to the cheap gorilla masks from costume shops or variety stores. The cables controlling his sophisticated, human-like expressions are all neatly tucked into the back of the suit, running out through a leg. There is an audible gasp of appreciation from everyone present as they behold the real star of the picture, the new King Kong!

The bear fur looks fantastic; the high crest of the head rises above the massive shoulder, but the rump sticks out a little too much. Rick's eyes seem incredibly small under the large, overhanging brows, giving an altogether comical look compared to the rest of the costume, but this discrepancy will later be corrected with large, brown scleral contact lenses that fit over the whites of the eye. Aside from that, the appearance of Kong seems flawless. The Italians, however, are not content, and they swarm all over Rick with brushes, combs and cans of hairspray. At one point, the fumes from the spray cans threaten to asphyxiate him and he staggers forward on the verge of collapse, saying "Mmphh, gimme some air! Gimme the tube fa-Chrissake!"

Rick has anticipated there might be some breathing difficulties inside the mask and has provided himself with a soft plastic breathing tube. It's inserted into the mouth of the gorilla mask and pushed up to reach Rick's own mouth, which is somewhere in the vicinity of Kong's nose. From this point on, Kong will appear to be holding a clear plastic cigar in his mouth between takes.

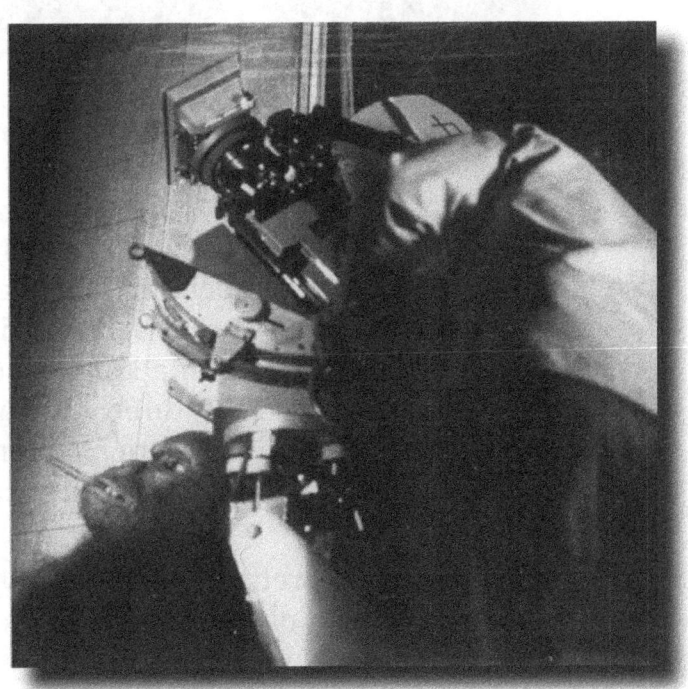

King Kong with breathing tube in the miniature tanker

As Kong finally steps up onto the platform and strides forward over his miniature world, the arc lamps are lit, one by one, and soon eight or nine electrical monsters are ablaze, illuminating the stage below. A loud crack and buzz announces the workings of the front-projection machine that smokes and puffs, and the Director, John Guillermin, a thin, intrepid Englishman, shouts his soon-to-be-familiar "Rayh-t, Action!"

John Guillermin and Dick Kline survey the miniature jungle

As Kong marches out over his world, an immense panorama of towering peaks and jungle stretch out behind him. The Kauai horizon is a beautiful mixture of blues, greens and browns, blended together in an awe-inspiring spectacle. Kong looks every inch a king as he dwarfs the rocks and trees around him, waking from a forty-three year slumber and once more casting his shadow across the history of motion picture art. At that precise moment I begin to contemplate various Hitchcockian schemes for the elimination of Mr Baker.

It soon becomes apparent, though, that I will be 'warming the bench' for quite some time. Instead of succumbing to the discomforts of the suit, Rick seems to revel in it! I will just have to wait my turn.

I attempt to console myself by seeking access to the dizzying heights of the sound stage. An intricate network of catwalks and ladders traverses the ceiling at least eighty feet above the concrete floor. Obviously, the higher superstructure serves a practical purpose, namely a grid for hanging lights or other equipment, but I am quite content thinking of it as a circus big-top. I notice that the only apparent access to this unexplored world seems to be straight up, using narrow ladders set against the wall. I am still new on the job and reluctant to attract attention to myself. I hear alarming tales about the wrath of the various labor unions and decide not to tempt fate. Then, behind the front-projection screen, I spot a stairway that traverses the entire rear wall of the sound stage on a diagonal incline.

As nonchalantly as possible, I stroll toward the screen and casually disappear behind it, my heart pounding with excitement. The stairway is truly awesome in its span and the height to which it rises. It also seems incredibly flimsy, being attached to the wall only on one side, and its metal construction offers little comfort as it jiggles with each mounting step. The concrete floor to my right gradually becomes smaller and smaller as I climb the staircase. Above me the lights on the miniature set glimmer over the top of the screen as I mount the stairway in shadow, carefully feeling each step through my shoe lest I make some fatal miscalculation. Finally, I emerge into the bright light of the arc lamps smoking far below and marvel at what I see. I grip the dirty, dusty, railing with my sweaty palms. The miniature set seems like an isolated island of earth adrift in darkness, illuminated by several little suns nearby. I imagine a scene in a screenplay of my own:

EXT. MOUNTAIN PEAK – NIGHT

The great beast sniffs the warm wind, rising up to its mountain lair from the steamy jungles far below. His huge hand-paw reaches up to swipe at nothing in particular. He snorts through his great nostrils as his brown eyes focus on a tiny clearing in the jungle swamp.

He cannot remember his own kind. There is only the great snake, and one of them must perish. Then the hairless two-leggeds came, building a great wall to keep him from the rest of the island. They are small but make other creatures fetch and carry for them; some they kill to eat. Alone, they are easy prey, but when they run together they are shrewd and deadly.

Friday March 26

When I report on Stage 27 this morning, Nate Haggard approaches me with an inscrutable grin. My chief impression is that either 1) we are about to share a private joke or 2) he knows I'm in for an unusual experience.

"Today," he says.

"Today?"

"They're gonna put you in the suit."

"You mean I'll be on camera?"

"Naw, they just wanna see if it fits."

Obviously Nate knows how eager I am to get into the gorilla suit and play the role of King Kong in any way I can, and he enjoys teasing me about my ambitions. I've been hanging around the set for almost a week now, trying not to get in anybody's way and make myself as inconspicuous as possible. No one has bothered to introduce me to the Director. Today, though, I decide to be bold and make my presence known.

John Guillermin, of *Towering Inferno* fame, is busy discussing Kong's walk with Rick, who is sitting on a wooden box (referred to in the film business as 'an apple box') and is wearing the complete Kong suit, minus the head. Mr Guillermin has the reputation of being an extremely demanding director, not above the use of pyrotechnical profanity whenever he is displeased. I overhear grumblings by subordinates in the commissary, but they all begrudgingly grant him their respect. In short, it seems the man knows his business and how to exact cooperation. I approach him with what I feel is the proper measure of awe and apprehension, being impressed with the way he often snaps the unwilling studio horde into shape. He smokes his pipe with the stem of his briar clenched tightly between his teeth as if he were sailing through a perpetual typhoon. He chooses casual attire, wearing slight variations of the same ensemble every day – brown suede shoes, chino pants and a knitted, short-sleeved sport shirt. His thin frame of medium height gives him a wiry, athletic appearance, and his facial features are characteristically British – he has prominent facial bones and gray-streaked, wavy hair brushed back against his head in 'old boy' fashion. A deep tan gives him the look of a weathered destroyer commander in the Royal Navy, and I can just see him, standing on the bridge of his burning ship with John Mills, tensely waiting for the inevitable torpedo from a German U-Boat. My reverie, however, is interrupted by Mr Guillermin's dialogue with Rick:

"Rayh-t. Well Rick, I believe Kong should walk more, well, standing up. Could we have him standing erect like a man, rather than have him crouching over like an ape?"

"Well, that's what I was trying to do, John, but the suit was made with the movement of the animal in mind. If I try to stand up too much, the butt's going to stick out."

Being an actor, I immediately know what the Director is talking about and decide to introduce myself without delay.

"Excuse me, Mr Guillermin. My name is Will Shephard, and if you're wondering what I'm doing here, I'm the second gorilla – Kong, I mean."

"Oh yeah," says Rick, waving a hairy paw at me, "I forgot."

I accept Rick's explanation of the introductory oversight and shake hands with Mr Guillermin who regards me with the amused expression of someone who meets Mickey Mouse for the first time. Having thus scored a major coup of professional strategy, I retire to a folding canvas chair nearby and ruminate over the subject matter under discussion.

Obviously Kong doesn't walk (or move) like a gorilla. No gorillas grow to be forty feet tall! In addition, he is imaginary, a uniquely American mythic creature, a manifestation of the human psyche that doesn't conform to any zoological fact or natural phenomenon. What's more, he is seen through the particular lens of American culture and society.

Why is Kong such a classic movie monster? He was certainly the first of his kind, but many film monsters have been created and destroyed since he first lumbered across movie screens in 1933 at the height of the Great Depression. It could be argued Kong is the most human, yet inhuman, monster ever imagined. He is pure myth. The story of King Kong has been a motion picture icon ever since Merian C Cooper and Ernest B Shoedsack came up with the idea. Kong is given the human weaknesses of the swarming mass of miniature life that watches him perched hopelessly on top of the Empire State building. Why does he develop a strong attachment to a pretty female human (pretty to us)? As Carl Denham says in the original 1933 *King Kong* script by James Creelman and Ruth Rose, "The beast was a tough guy, too. He could lick the world, but when he met beauty, she got him; he went soft, he forgot his wisdom, and the little guys got him."

I am lost in my thoughts for some time when Nate tells me to report to Stage 15 for a costume fitting. It's only a question of crossing the street on the studio lot to an adjacent building, but I feel as if I am about to enter another world. Stage 15 is practically bare except for a number of workers making miniature rubber and plastic trees. At one end, a large cyclorama of mountains and plains is being painted, and, on the other, an enormous construction of styrofoam and wood is being erected. There is one small portable dressing room on the stage, and two of the Italians are waiting for me, smiling beside their cart of Kong accessories – costumes, masks and cables. I'm eager to get into the suit, so I hurry into the dressing room and strip down to my underwear. Paolo and Isidoro squeeze into the dressing room with the inner suit and help me into the padding by reaching up and guiding my feet through the leggings. Rick and I are going to depend a great deal on these two men in the coming months. Both are of medium height, a little overweight, and they give a friendly feeling to that cramped little room. Paolo is in his forties, has graying curly hair, and wears bowling shoes. He's a tailor by trade who emigrated to the US and speaks English with a charming accent. Isidoro looks younger, about thirty-five, and he is continually wiping his brown wavy hair back from his tinted glasses. He doesn't speak much English since he just came over to work with Rambaldi on the Kong suits, but we manage to communicate in broken French.

The gorilla suits, ready and waiting

I wonder if it's true that all Italians are opera singers at heart, so – as they are about to finish dressing me in the outer suit of bear hide – I begin a loud chorus of 'Ridi, Pagliaccio ...' Sure enough, they pick up the cue and finish the chorus together in unison, 'Sul tuo amore infranto!' I am in such good spirits that I begin to 'Charleston' as soon as I am completely suited up as Kong. The men working on the rubber trees drop their paint brushes. I am having such a good time I don't stop to think what a dancing gorilla must look like. Soon enough, though, I begin to slow down when I realize I'm trapped. There is no way in the world I can get out of the suit by myself in case of an emergency. My hands are deep inside the arm extensions, and I am virtually helpless. My eyes, peeping through the mask, are the only part of me in contact with the outside. All of a sudden, I become short of breath, and ripples of panic spread through me. A memory of a movie I'd seen as a child in the 50s flashes through my mind.

In a sword-and-sandal Egyptian epic popular at the time, a woman was being tortured to reveal the identity of someone who had tried to assassinate the Pharaoh. A huge, two-ton granite block had been cut in half horizontally, and parts of it had been hollowed out to accommodate the shape of a human being lying flat with arms outstretched. One half of the stone block was suspended over the other by several heavy ropes, and when it was lowered, only the hands of the victim protruded from the living tomb. I remembered the woman's frantic screams and the agony in her twitching hands. I felt trapped with her inside the massive darkness, unable to move, with a ton of granite only inches away from my face and body.

Fortunately I succeed in mastering my panic before anyone notices something strange is going on inside the suit. I am breathing my own exhalations and starting to feel dizzy; then I remember the plastic breathing tube. Bob Mills carefully cleans the tube with alcohol, taking ever so long to make it sanitary while I am in dire need of fresh air. Finally, the jaws of the mask are pried open, and the tube is inserted, to my intense relief.

"Wait a minute – I've got to scratch this itch!"

As I am breathing easier and overcoming my temporary panic, I happen to glance at a mirror on the make-up table, and I nearly faint. I am completely unrecognizable to myself! Oh, I expected to look different in a gorilla suit, but I'm not prepared for the bizarre metamorphosis that has taken place. Not a shred of me is apparent. I am lost inside Kong, and whatever I do, he does.

Rambaldi and Mario Chiari suddenly appear from behind a grove of miniature artificial trees, making strange faces as they discuss how I look in the suit. Rambaldi's lips are more tightly pursed than ever; in fact, his mouth seems to wrinkle up and disappear under his bushy black eyebrows. I gather from the tone and inflection of their conversation that they are not entirely pleased. Rick is perhaps a little larger in the butt and legs, and the suit had been custom tailored for him. Why hasn't anybody fitted me for a suit as well? The knees on the suit are a bit baggy on me, and the crotch sags. Rambaldi keeps shaking his head and making faces as if he'd just bitten into a tainted calzone. As Paolo and Isidoro help me out of the suit, a laborious process that takes anywhere from thirty to forty minutes, I can't help noticing that I'm drenched with sweat. I hear there had been talk of installing a cooling system in the suit at one point, but the actor's health or comfort is of no particular concern to the Producer – unless we interrupt the production schedule by passing out.

Monday March 29

'Refined' is a word that comes to mind whenever I think of William Kronick, Mr Guillermin's Second Unit Director. His job is to film the action sequences – helicopters taking off, attacks from 'natives', fights with giant snakes etc – in addition to re-takes, which Mr Guillermin is too busy to bother with. Polite yet aloof, intelligent yet cool, affable yet patronizing – these are the qualities of William Kronick when I first meet him. I even go so far as to think we have something in common; we're both standing around, watching someone else do the main work. I really don't know how *he* feels about it, but the long periods of inactivity are very trying for me, despite the fact that I am being paid to do nothing. Kronick doesn't seem very old, though the wisps of hair around his temples are beginning to gray. His high forehead, accentuated by his shining bald head and aquiline nose, give his features a slightly Roman look, but his blue-gray eyes and facial bone structure suggest more of a northeastern European heritage.

As a fellow member of the B-team, I try various topics of conversation with him, hoping to pass the time a little more quickly. When I ask him questions about the film, his answers are short and to the point. As to what he thinks will be happening in future work on the film, he insists he doesn't have the slightest idea. I confess I feel like a fool, dogging the man's heels with a styrofoam cup of coffee in my hands, but Mr Kronick never seems to stand on ceremony when he tires of my attempts at friendly chatter. If there is the briefest lull in our conversation, or perhaps even when I am in the middle of a sentence, he simply turns on his heel and walks away. Sometimes his hand trembles ever so slightly as he raises a heavily creamed coffee to his lips. Bill Kronick carries himself with poise and dignity, but his ironic smile often gives me the impression of a man who is inwardly pacing, back and forth, like a tiger in a cage.

When I was still teaching at the college near Los Feliz Boulevard in Hollywood, I often took hikes in nearby Griffith Park to shake the academic dust from my shoes. One day, having climbed to the top of Mount Hollywood and begun my descent on the other side, I came upon an old wire fence in the middle of some extremely dense foliage. Having no regard for fences other than as a brief inconvenience, I climbed a tree and swung myself over, landing on the other side on a piece of concrete. A thick carpet of leaves had covered the stone-like surface, and my hard landing was a surprise. Whatever grounds I had stumbled on were almost completely obscured by the growth of foliage that seemed to have been left unattended for many years. Feeling my way upon a path, I descended a small flight of concrete steps and found myself confronted by row upon row of small, empty cages whose metal frames and cage wires had turned a deep, reddish brown, having rusted in the elements. Turning around, I discovered a tall, wire-mesh cage as big as a two- or three-storey house. It must have been an aviary for rare and exotic birds. I imagined I could hear the ghostly cries of brilliantly plumed parrots, toucans, kingfishers and birds of paradise in the high-vaulted, open-air confinement where they had lived and died, far from their natural habitat. I then followed another path that began as a gradual incline up the side of a hill, and came upon a series of heavy metal doors set in outcropping structures of concrete and stone. One door was slightly ajar and I entered cautiously. I found myself in a narrow passage and began to descend a flight of stairs; the rise and tread of each step was greater than any used for human movement. As I descended, I noticed a heavy cage door suspended by a cable above my head. It was obviously intended to seal off the passageway in some emergency, though for what reason I couldn't say. At length, I passed through a low aperture at the foot of the steps and found myself in a cave-like structure that was obviously man-made, but fashioned to give the appearance of a natural setting. The floor of the cave extended only a few yards then dropped off into a deep moat. On the other side of the moat the wall rose several yards, and there was an iron railing and another path that ran along beside it. Immediately I realized I had stumbled into an abandoned zoo. Yes – the smaller cages, the aviary – and now I was standing in a large animal cage reserved for major predators such as lions or tigers. How often, as a child, I had gazed down across the safety of the railing, high walls and moat at dangerous wild animals only a few yards away. Now I felt strangely different. A feeling of sadness came over me for those missing animals that had once been the objects of our amusement.

It is as if our conquering or subduing these powerful animals was designed to make our human lives seem, by comparison, so much grander. Though we are no match for their natural strength and their ability to kill us with a swipe of a powerful claw, we feel superior because of our guile and cleverness. As Carl Denham says in the 1933 classic when Kong has been knocked out by gas bombs:

Carl Denham: Why, the whole world will pay to see this.

Captain Englehorn: No chains will ever hold that.

Carl Denham: We'll give him more than chains. He's always been king of his world, but we'll teach him fear ...

Wednesday March 31

Today, while Rick is busy with Guillermin and the First Unit, Bill Kronik is assigned to do some front-screen tests on Stage 27, using me in Rick's old gorilla suit, the one with the big belly and synthetic hair. Harold Wellman, the Second Unit cameraman, sits regally in his folding wooden director's chair as subordinates busy about, adjusting the camera, mirrors and projection machine. Wellman is a tall, older man, very well dressed in slacks, a long-sleeved, wide-collared quiana shirt, and a cravat. His appearance is impeccable and dignified, as though his patriarchal demeanor puts him on a plane well above the scuffling humanity all around him. Rafael Elortegui, a young Cuban expatriate, is functioning as AD for the Second Unit, though he is technically only a trainee. He has already demonstrated such reliability, together with a good measure of tact and a sense of humor, that he's been given the full responsibilities of the position without, of course, the formal title and commensurate salary. These are the key collaborators I am to work with as I make my on-camera debut as Kong 2, or 'Kong, too' as I am sometimes called.

Only Paolo is present to help me into the suit, the other Italians being occupied elsewhere with the First Unit. Paolo embodies old-world traditions of modesty, graciousness and intelligence that make him a joy to work with. He seems to be the only one among his colleagues who has any sympathy for the man in the gorilla suit, and I need sympathy because the old suit is a cumbersome annoyance after the superior, streamlined model worn by Rick. The end result will be the same – sweat and exhaustion – but this one is heavier to lug around.

"Okay, Weel, you fill awright?" asks Paolo. "How come-a you not work wit de First-a Unity?"

"Search me, Paolo," I reply. "Thanks, I feel fine, but haven't we got another one of the new suits I could wear?"

"Ahm-a sorry, Weel. Rambaldi say we only work on-a one suit now. What I can say? Hey, you wanna de glovus on now, or you wanna wait?"

"The what?" I ask.

"De glovus, Weel, de glovus. Aw you must-a plees pay attention."

"Are you talking about the arm extensions?"

"Yeah, sure."

"Alright, let's put 'em on."

After I've been completely suited up except for the head, Bob Mills sits me down and blackens my face with the compound of dark, diatomaceous earth.

Gorilla eyes! Now I've just got to wait for the rest of my face to be blackened

"This stuff will come off easily with 'Double Depth'," he tells me.

"Double Depth?"

"Yeah, it's a cleansing cream – the best you can get. I have some here in my make-up box."

"Fine. I'll see you the moment I come off camera."

The lights are set, the front-projection machine begins huffing and puffing, and I'm asked to stand on two apple boxes, each sixteen inches wide, in order for Mr Wellman to get me into focus. The heat under the lights is excruciating, and the head hasn't even been put on yet. More lights are turned on, and as they sputter and smoke, an electrician calls out to me from the top of one of the fifteen-foot lighting towers.

"Hey, man, turn your eyes away from the light. Don't look at it or you'll go blind!"

"Where'd they get this suit?" Kronick shouts. "It looks like an old, moth-eaten bearskin rug, and look at that belly. Kong looks pregnant!"

Everyone seems to have a good laugh at Kronick's remark except for Rafael, who is busy explaining to the Director that there is only one good suit for now. Meanwhile, I am busy cooking in my own sweat and can't see the humor in the moment.

Finally, the gorilla head is attached, and the temperature in the suit seems to go up another twenty degrees. I'm trying to keep my balance on the narrow boxes, and I'm finding it more and more difficult to breathe. I previously edged the jaws of the mask open with a piece of wood, but the heat is so great inside the mask that sweat is pouring down my face and into my eyes, which are stinging.

"Okay, Rick, here's what I want you to do," shouts Kronick.

"THSSUS WLL, WLL – UHMM THU."

"What – what's he saying?" asks Kronick.

"It's Will – Will is inside the suit," says Rafael.

"What the hell! How am I supposed to know the difference? Okay, okay. Awright, Will, here's what I want you to do – you're in the foreground, and we'll be projecting a waterfall up on the screen behind you."

('Good God, what torture,' I thought.)

"Now I want you to turn slowly from the left to the right – that's it, but don't fall off the apple boxes. Make him proud, 'The Proud Gorilla'. Hey, wait a minute – why is his mouth open? His jaw looks dislocated!"

"AHH CNNT BREVV WIF IT CLOSS."

"He says he can't breathe with it closed," says Rafael.

"Oh, awright, keep it open. Let's roll 'em – Action!"

I pirouette on the apple boxes, over and over, and take after take I look behind me to see the waterfall go backwards as the plate is rewound. That cool waterfall rushing uphill seems a million miles away, but my sweat still obeys the laws of gravity and begins to form puddles in my gorilla feet.

"Action! Okay, Will, now turn slowly and look at the waterfall. That's it – now, back at me. Look down at my knees – now high, higher. Move the arms, yeah. Get that left arm up in front of your chest – we don't wanna see your shag carpet. Cut!"

We finish at seven o'clock that night, and Paolo mercifully wipes the sweat out of my eyes with tissue after tissue. Bob Mills has already gone home, though, and I have nothing to take the make-up off with, so I drive home with my blackened face and collapse on the bed in my apartment without trying to remove the make-up.

Monday April 5

A half-ton of water rushes down a vertical slide, smashes into a shovel-like basin and explodes onto a set piece of a ship at sea. Jeff Bridges as 'Jack Prescott' carefully lifts the canvas cover of a lifeboat where he's been hiding and is deluged by a combination of fire hoses and waves from the thirty-foot high holding tanks. The deck of the ship pitches and rolls by the manipulation of huge, hydraulic machinery underneath, and John Guillermin rides out the storm strapped to his chair in the camera boom together with his cinematographer, Dick Kline. Their yellow sou'westers help keep them partially dry, and only the most delicate mist and spray settle on the gang of spectators assembled on Stage 14 to watch the aquatic display.

Soon it's all over. The water ceases its surge, the work lights come on, and the crew begins to wade around in the residue. Practically everyone is wearing knee-high rubber boots except for those of us who have been watching from a wooden platform well out of harm's way.

I've never witnessed such spectacular effects before, and I'm completely under the spell of what is sometimes referred to as 'movie magic' even though I can see how it's done. God, how I'd loved to have done Jeff Bridges' role in the foregoing scene! Thoughts of the chariot race in *Ben Hur*, the colossal sets of D W Griffith's *Intolerance* and my own Palace of Fine Arts experience in San Francisco crowd into my mind all at once. Sometimes the technical set-ups between takes seem to take forever, but for anyone who has ever imagined sailing the seven seas, flying over mountain-tops on a magic carpet, or discovering lost worlds hidden deep in the jungles or high on unreachable plateaux, there is no greater fascination than the great special effects of the fabulous movies.

As I cross the boundary between the magic of Stage 14 and the harsh reality of the outside lot, the bright sun hurts my eyes, and my inner fantasy world is shattered. I walk down the narrow roadway towards the Model Shop to keep an appointment with Isidoro, who is preparing to cast a life mask of my head and face.

When I arrive, I notice a white plaster bust of Rick already serving as a model on which the mechanical workings of the Kong mask are taking shape. There, on a sculptor's stand in the tiny, dusty office of Carlo Rambaldi, a rubber gorilla mask is being fitted with soldered pieces of wire that are to form the mechanical framework for Kong's facial expressions. Rick had told me earlier that Rambaldi's initial plan was to have a system of electronically powered, remote-control devices in the mask that would give Kong his human appeal. Frankly, I'm horrified at the thought of having electrical components so close to the face of man in the suit. What if the mask accidentally short-circuits and catches fire?

Fortunately, the cost of the electrical system makes it impractical, so the designer has had to settle for manual manipulation. As I enter the shop, the Italians are hunched over their cables and levers, which look like an elaborate system for flushing every toilet on the lot simultaneously. Rambaldi paces back and forth with his familiar hunted expression, nervously lipping a cigarette. Isidoro, dressed in a sweat-stained T-shirt and dirty work pants, keeps wiping his hair back from his tinted glasses that are fogging up with the intensity of his concentration. Paolo, on the other hand, skips around the dustbin of the shop in his now-tattered bowling shoes, oblivious to the accumulating debris as long as he's snipping bear hide with his tailor's shears and gleefully discarding the scraps on the floor. Rick lounges on a filthy sofa that gives off a cloud of dust whenever he moves. He regards me with a playful grin.

"So they're gonna brick up your face, eh?"

"That's what I'm told," I say.

"You've got nothing to worry about," he says, smiling with elfish delight. "But, you know, there was this make-up man, a real psycho. Well, he puts plaster all over this guy's head to make a life mask, then he goes off and forgets about him. By the time he gets back, the stuff is hard as stone, and this make-up man has forgotten to leave a seam around the edge so he can take the mold off. He tells the guy not to worry."

Rick interrupts himself, doubling over with laughter. When he gains control again, he continues:

"Well, he leaves the room and comes back with a hammer and a chisel, and he starts to pound away at this guy's head. The guy jumps out of the chair and crashes into the doorway, trying to get away. Somehow, he manages to find his way outside and, blind as a bat, he starts running down the road, pursued by this nutcase waving the hammer and chisel."

Rick laughs, watching to see my reaction. Sure enough, I look around me at the shop and begin to feel very uncomfortable.

"That's a good one," I say.

He's having me on, teasing me – isn't he? I sit down on the edge of the couch, and Isidoro smiles, rubbing his hands together. His eyes twinkle behind his tinted glasses. My shirt is carefully hung up on the closet door, and my personal effects – keys, wallet, change – are deposited in a manila envelope (for my next of kin?). I take comfort from the fact that everyone else is going about their business in the shop with no apparent concern over what is about to happen to me. Isidoro dons a pair of surgical gloves and proceeds to mix a bucketful of white, pasty material with water.

"What's that?" I ask, pointing at the mixture.

"Izzy," Rick says. "Will wants to know what you're mixing."

"Eh? Alginato!"

"It's alginate. Don't worry," Rick tells me. "Dentists use it to make impressions of people's teeth. It's a soft, rubbery material that'll make an impression of your face and then slip right off. The only thing you have to worry about is losing your eyebrows."

Rick laughs again and hands me some Vaseline to smear on my eyebrows. I'm given a rubber skullcap to put over my hair, and Isidoro begins to paste the alginate on the back of my head as I sit on the edge of the couch. I feel a familiar rush of panic as the stuff is spread over my mouth and eyes, but I can still see a little light behind my eyelids. Then Isidoro applies the second coat and I'm immersed in darkness. Rick tells me to blow hard through my nostrils whenever I want to clear my breathing passages, and I'm going at it as hard as I can.

Then suddenly my momentary panic is gone. I feel the weight of the alginate as it hardens on my face, and then the warmth it generates induces me to doze off. I don't know how long I actually nap in the confinement of the mask, but eventually I become aware that Rick is gently shaking me and talking to me:

"Wakey wakey, Willy-Boy. Now you've got to sit up and let us take this chamber pot off your head."

Rick helps me up to a sitting position on the couch, and Isidoro starts to remove the alginate mold. As soon as it's off, Rick hands me a cold Dr Pepper he has just bought from the snack truck parked outside the shop. He smiles and raises his own Dr Pepper, toasting my initiation into the world of film gorilla men.

"Well, Willy, you came through with flying colors," he says.

"Thanks, Rick, and believe me when I say I won't forget all you've done for me." I give him a meaningful look.

I have just undergone a rite of passage, an initiation, into a select group, an elite corps of men who have made their living in the movies dressed as gorillas. Rick explains to me that most of the former greats were specialist stunt men who made their own suits. As Rick recites the honor roll, including the late Janos Prohaska, Charlie Gemora and Crash Corrigan, I see film-clip after film-clip pass before my eyes. I remember, when I was a child, a fantastic scene from the movie serial 'Tim Tyler and the Jungle Patrol' where a group of ferocious gorillas throw boulders at white hunters who invade their territory in search of ivory. I remember Buster Crabbe, fighting a gorilla that had a horn growing out of its head in one of the 'Flash Gordon' serials. And, as Rick says, "Who can forget Charlie Gemora's performance as the killer ape in *Murders in the Rue Morgue?*"

Rick tells me that the great gorilla men of the past had no ready format for their work – they just set about constructing elaborate suits and then ambled across the screen. There was no accepted technique of gorilla portrayal: they just seemed to have the talent for it. In reality, of course, the gorilla is a relatively gentle animal, a vegetarian with no desire to deflower human virgins, but the movie gorilla is something different: a mirror of the human condition, as all screen monsters are.

Rick also remembers one fellow, a security guard in Chicago and a former stunt man, who claimed to have portrayed the original King Kong in 1933, despite the fact that everyone knows that Kong was an eighteen-inch tall model animated through the process of stop-motion photography. Nevertheless, the elderly guard periodically hauled out a moth-eaten gorilla suit and explained how he became 'The Eighth Wonder of the World'.

"I had rubber suction cups on my shoes when I climbed the Empire State Building," he used to say.

Thursday April 8

The bizarre experience of having my head encased in alginate is a walk in the park compared to what awaits me as I'm driving out to El Monte to be fitted for Kong's eyes – large, scleral contact lenses that are filled with saline solution and fitted on the whites of the eyes. I've seen them on Rick, and he looks positively inhuman; if he had long, straight whiskers under his nose he would resemble a seal. The large, brown gorilla eyes have a liquid, sentimental appearance, and as far as I know they've never been used by gorilla-men before. Watching Rick's attempts to put them on was an agonizing experience. Rick needed several attempts to place the lenses, filled with saline solution, under his upper and lower eyelid. For instance, in order to insert the left lens, Rick had to bend over, reach over the top of his head with his right hand and raise the upper left eyelid. Holding the cup-shaped lens carefully in his left hand to keep from spilling the solution, he inserted the lens under his upper left lid and pushed it up with his thumb as far as it would go. Then he pulled his upper left lid down over the lens like a window shade and slipped his bottom lid over the lower side of the lens. It was very disturbing to watch. His eyes became more and more bloodshot with each try, and he shed copious tears in the process.

My palms are wet and sticky on the steering wheel as I drive East along Highway 10. I've never worn glasses and am uneasy at the thought of anything touching my eyes. Every time I've witnessed the simplest putting in or taking out of contact lenses, I have inwardly writhed. I can think of no torture more agonizing, with the possible exception of a finger probing my navel. As I pull into the small parking lot beside the optometrist's office, I try to compose myself.

Dr Solon Braff is one of a vanishing breed of optometrists who still make scleral contacts, no doubt on consignments from TV or motion picture companies. His waiting room has a modest 'early motel' décor. The yellow vinyl couch and the pastel-painted walls give a cheery, antiseptic feeling to the waiting room. The lady in white behind the glass partition asks me to be seated, and I begin nervously perusing a copy of *Time* magazine. Dr Braff soon appears in the doorway and ushers me into a narrow examination room just inside the office door. The room is odd. It's fairly long and narrow, jutting away from the administrative offices at a peculiar angle. Maybe it's my imagination, but the structure of the examination room seems to suggest something along the lines of the famous 'Winchester Mystery House' where halls lead nowhere, stairways go up into the ceiling, and doors open on blank walls or a precipitous drop to the lawn outside.

Dr Braff is a jovial man, slightly stout and dressed in a physician's white coat. His hands are large with orange freckles, and he wears rimless glasses.

"How are things on King Kong?" he asks.

"Oh, fine – fine," I reply.

"Have you ever worn contact lenses before?"

"No."

"Doesn't really matter," he says. "We'll just give you a little examination and see how your eyes are."

The examination is straightforward and I try hard not to betray my mounting anxiety. Rick told me that Dr Braff is pretty matter-of-fact about the whole thing. "He just shoves the lenses in and pops them out," he'd said.

"Will they hurt much?" I ask.

"Hurt? No siree – won't hurt at all," says Dr Braff.

After making notations about my eyes, he removes a clear plastic lens from a selection of different sizes and gives me a paper towel.

"Now just lean forward. I'm going to do this for you, but please pay attention. All right! We just lift the upper lid, insert the lens – now look up, look down. There we are."

It all happened quite rapidly. Before I knew it, something is inserted under the lid of my right eye. When I open it, I seem to be looking through a fishbowl. There is no discomfort exactly, but I begin to feel a little strange. I feel even stranger when the second lens is inserted, and I'm looking through stereoscopic fishbowls. My toes and fingers begin to tingle, and I begin to sweat.

"Doctor," I say, "I'm beginning to feel a little funny."

"That's all right, son, we all feel a little funny now and then."

"No, I mean ..."

"Really? Well just lean forward a little more. Any better?"

"No-o-o, I think it's the lenses."

"Here, let's take 'em out."

(Plop – Plop)

"I'm still dizzy."

"Well, maybe you better come into another room and lie down for a minute."

Dr Braff leads me to another room, and I lie down on the carpet. I look up at the little holes in the ceiling panels. Little black holes? Suddenly I'm falling through darkness and landing back in my childhood nightmare:

I'm riding down the valley of giant, crashing boulders, on a big red plastic fork, bouncing vertically along a taut piece of string. Other large, riderless forks are also bouncing along the string, but they're frequently shattered when the mountainous boulders crash together just in front or behind me.

"Feeing any better?"

I become aware that Dr Braff is standing over me.

"You know," he says as he helps me to my feet, "nothing like this has happened for at least twenty-five years. The last time it happened, I was fitting a big, two-hundred-and-fifty pound policeman for lenses back in

1951. As soon as I put 'em in, he started to pass out, just like you."

When I return to the studio late in the afternoon, Rick asks me how the fitting went. I give a vague answer, neglecting any of the specifics. The lenses need to be ground to fit my vision, and then given their brown appearance. In a few weeks I'll have to return to El Monte and repeat the whole process.

I spend the rest of the day wandering around the lot and finally approach the construction shop where the huge, forty-foot mechanical Kong is being assembled at a cost of several million dollars. Whether it will ever be fully functional in the film is a purely speculative matter. It probably doesn't really matter: Mr De Laurentiis is paying for millions of dollars worth of the best advance publicity he can buy.

As I look at the hydraulic system and the metal skeleton stretched out on the floor, I feel a twinge of sympathy, not knowing how much, if any, of Kong I will play and what I will make of it. At the far end of the warehouse, Kong's giant head and torso are taking shape in large blocks of styrofoam.

The styrofoam head and shoulders dwarfs the warehouse

37

This thing is costing several million dollars, but will it ever work?

I pass back by the Model Shop to see if my life mask has been finished, and there it is on the end of a wooden shaft, like a head impaled on a spear. My hairless head and face look hard, like they belong to some ancient military commander who spent his life fighting scorpions and bandits in an unforgiving desert.

Friday April 9

Rain today. The streets are slick as I drive to the studio. It seems like typical April weather for most parts of the country, but no weather in Los Angeles is ever typical. Stage 27 is cold and damp like an underground cavern. The electricians on the arc lamps and other lighting instruments are the only ones who seem to be keeping warm. I also learn that coffee is a diuretic. I suppose I never really appreciated that fact until I have to run through the rain, three times in one hour, to the rest rooms outside the sound stage. Rick and I fantasize about having a mobile home parked just outside the sound stage, but gorilla men have to sprint for distant urinals like everybody else.

Fortunately, Jessica Lange isn't on call today, and I inherit a portable dressing room, usually reserved for stars or featured actors, that is roughly eight feet square. Rick is busy somewhere else, and I have the dressing room all to myself. It's warm and has its own charm as a getaway on the sound stage – knotty-pine walls, red imitation-leather couch and armchair, table lamps, make-up desk and mirror – all looking like they belong to another era. A few of Jessica's shells and portions of a grass skirt lie scattered about the room, but, overall, the place looks like something Clark Gable or Myrna Loy might've once used. Outside on the sound stage, tests are being filmed with a full-scale, mechanical, gorilla arm and hand which is mounted on cranes in front of the blue screen. Many problems have come up with the complex system that animates the gargantuan wrist, hand and fingers. It seems the whole contraption keeps breaking down. The heavy latex hand is tied onto its metal frame with ropes, a temporary arrangement in order for the crew to get at the working parts when the whole thing collapses.

Nothing is safe in the path of that ponderous gorilla hand and arm. Sawhorses, styrofoam rocks and prop trees are crushed when the big hand falls. Sometimes, even the crew has to run for it.

Stand back before the big hand gets you!

One imaginative idea had been for the giant hand to be controlled by a single man, wearing an elaborate console strapped to his body with electrical cables running along his arm to mechanical fingers that fit over his own. I suppose the idea is to mimic the mechanical apparatus used in handling dangerous chemicals, but the size and weight of the Kong machinery make it impractical. The big hand, wrist and arm are now controlled by electrical switches and rheostats mounted on a table console, off-camera – a more elaborate version of the way the Italians operate Kong's facial expressions with their mechanical levers. An attractive blond stunt woman named Sunny has the hazardous task of riding up into the air in Kong's massive, mechanical grasp, while the special effects crew keep assuring her that nothing can go wrong. Supposedly, the fingers have built-in stops or safeguards to prevent them from injuring Sunny by squishing her like a ripe banana.

I can't help thinking what would happen if the arm and hand malfunction, throwing the poor woman across the sound stage. Joe Day, a special-effects man, assures me that the whole thing is foolproof: he uses an expression I've come to identify with the motion picture business, "It's a piece of cake. You could mail it in."

Later, Sunny drops by the dressing room for a visit because it's one of the few warm places on the sound stage, and we talk about the dangers of the big hand.

"Aren't you afraid something could go wrong?" I ask.

"No, not really. I've done more dangerous things, like falling out of buildings, being shot from a cannon, that sort of thing. Oh, I get pinched in the hand now and then, and I've got some pretty impressive bruises, but nothing special."

Our conversation becomes more animated as she talks about her trapeze work in the circus, but the stunt-coordinator looks in to tell her she's needed 'in the hand.' A few moments later, Federico drops in and we have a nice conversation about how things are going with the movie. I enjoy talking to him. He seems very relaxed and sympathizes with the difficulties I sometimes experience as Kong 2. His pleasant attitude is a welcome respite from my inactivity. Later, I decide to take a walk.

The rain has stopped, and as I walk outside I look up and notice jagged clouds racing across the sky like a pack of white wolves, the hair bristling on their backs. Southern California is often given to such celestial displays, Los Angeles in particular when the smog abates. It has long been the task of cinematographers to capture brilliant landscapes or panoramas and hold them like a bee in amber – those spectacles of nature that never fail to provoke awe and wonder in movie audiences. In a similar fashion, there are artificial spectacles created by motion pictures to stir and amaze audiences as well. One such fantasy is the Great Wall on Kong's Island, supposedly built by superstitious natives to keep back the inconceivable force that roams through dense jungles just beyond their primitively ordered world. Surely, in the story, these natives are not so foolish to believe any structure could actually prevent that monstrous power from breaking through that token partition if it really wanted to. But the wall itself, in the original film story and the present version, represents a functional barrier in nature, a shadow-line between light and darkness, between inspiration and insanity, between consciousness and the unconscious – where no-one may pass through and return unaltered.

For several days truckloads of lumber, fiberglass logs, hanging vines and plastic orchids have been collecting out on the back lot of MGM on Overland Avenue. For weeks, construction has been moving on towards the completion of a giant wall seventy feet tall, twenty feet wide, and a curved city block long. The scale is magnificent. It doesn't seem very impressive to begin with, just a lot of scaffolding, plywood and pilings, but as the day scheduled for shooting approaches, it begins to take on its fabulous character, rising from the ashes of past movie spectacles.

Federico drops in for a chat to the dressing-room that Rick and I are sharing

Wednesday April 14

Rambaldi, Paolo and Isidoro look like they've been up all night when I walk into the tiny office at the rear of the Model Shop. This morning they are all sporting overnight stubble, and their eyes have that bleary, pinkish-red hue above the bags of skin below. Several empty boxes of Winchell's Donuts lie on the floor, and a coffee urn has been brought in and set up on a shelf strewn with pieces of latex and bear hide. A whole new set of blueprints for the Kong suits and masks have cropped up on the wall. Paolo is furiously stitching up some pieces of bear hide with heavy black thread and a long needle, Isidoro sweats over levers and cables that kept breaking, and Rambaldi paces back and forth, chain-smoking and squinting to keep the smoke out of his eyes.

"Che cazzo!" says Rambaldi.

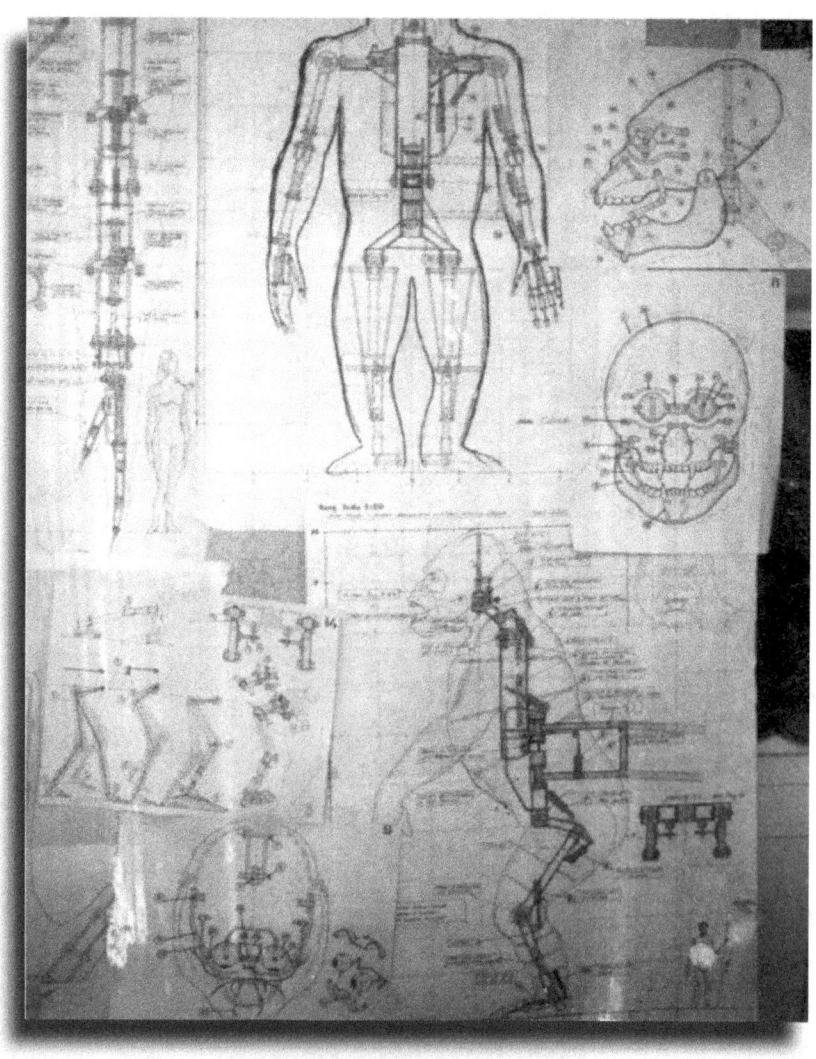

More blueprints, more changes

"Che testa di cazzo – cazzone!" echoes Isidoro.

"Hey, what's going on?" I ask.

Paolo replies: "Missa De Laurentiis, he call up yistidday afffanoon an' say he wanna de soot ready fo' today – issa impossible!"

At this point Rambaldi cuts in with a stream of Italian expletives.

Paola translates: "Rambaldi say dissa de las' time he stay uppa all night fo' anybody, an' he's-a right, too! Issa okay fo' Missa De Lauren' to make-a las' minute-a demans; he don' haffa do de work! I don' unnastan-a dees people! Why don' dey plan-a tings betta?"

"Porca la miseria," screams Isidoro as the cables break for the third time.

Kong's inner musculature and facial expressions have been completely reworked overnight by Rambaldi and his men, and they've done a very good job. Rambaldi is certainly the mechanical wizard he is made out to be. Kong has a completely new repertoire of facial expressions – eyebrows that go up and down, a mouth that can do everything but spit, and a nose that wrinkles, flaring the nostrils. The expressions in the mask are so incredibly human that even Rambaldi laughs as Isidoro manipulates the levers, making Kong go through a hilarious series of facial expressions.

One of Rick's earlier gorilla masks

Thursday April 15

The sky is gray and overcast again, and it seems unlikely that any shooting will take place on the Great Wall as planned. I drive onto the back lot to see how the work is going and notice several cars parked by the ruins of the French Village set. Today's call-sheet specifies some five hundred extras, dancers, and 'Ju-Ju men' (witchdoctors), but the First Unit crew seems to be the only personnel on hand. The set of the Great Wall looks fantastic. The skeletal structure I'd seen before is now completely transformed into an imposing edifice of pagan splendor. Apparently the original wall used in the 1933 classic was a leftover – a refurbished structure from Cecil B DeMille's Biblical epic *The King of Kings* made in 1927. It resembled a massive stone remnant from a lost civilization, the carved lintel above the giant double door looking vaguely Mayan in design. Kong's new wall, however, is made to look like a giant wooden construction of interwoven timbers and vines with tropical flora, a much more primitive structure. Scores of men in hard hats are climbing over the structure, which rises ominously in the early-morning gray.

The miniature Great Wall takes shape

The huge double door looks like several forest giants joined together, and the bolt which locks the gates – an enormous 'log' from a giant tree trunk – needs an entire section of the wall for support when not in use. Charcoal fires are smoldering all around, partly for visual effect and partly for warmth, and there is a peculiar smell in the air, a smell of incense. Little chunks of pressed wood and wax used for smoke effects give off a strangely aromatic odor, like that of a Russian Orthodox Church I once visited.

Friday April 16

In a motion picture company there is a very complex pecking order, but there are ways of ingratiating oneself in order to bypass the accepted code. For example, being classified as second-string 'talent', I am at the bottom of the pecking order, whereas Jessica Lange's stand-in, also at the bottom end, manages to elevate herself by rubbing up against men of the crew and engaging in a series of promiscuous back-rubs. Lest it sound like sour grapes on my part, I've noticed that women, in a predominantly male organization, are considered valuable even if they stand around doing nothing, whereas when I stand around doing nothing – through no fault of my own – I'm subjected to the jokes of those who take pleasure in reminding me that I'm only a second-string gorilla.

It's bad enough that Rambaldi and Chiari stand around making sour faces whenever I'm in one of the Kong suits, creating a spectacle of their disapproval, but the curly-headed Italian translator whose name, oddly enough, is Capra, puts on airs and tells everyone how *he* would direct the picture, referring to me as the 'stand-by gorilla' or Rick Baker's understudy.

On the sound stage even Bill Kronick comments on my status, poking fun at me.

"Are you familiar with the Russian opera, *Boris Godunov* by Mussorgsky?" he asks me.

"Yes," I say.

"Well, there's this pretender to the throne, a monk who claims to be the missing Tsarevich, who's known as 'The False Dimitri.' That's what I'll call you from now on, 'The False Dimitri'," he says, chuckling at his own joke.

Needless to say I am mortified, being intellectually pilloried by the Second Unit director.

I've just finished a test in the 'good' Kong suit when a call comes from the Producer's office, requesting 'the man in the suit' to please stand by while

Mr De Laurentiis brings some visitors down to see the ingenuity of the Kong suit. Someone says that the mystery guest is the president of Paramount Pictures, so I naturally honor my employer's request and sit in the suit for forty-five minutes until he arrives with his party in the Rolls Royce that he uses to drive around the lot.

Paolo kindly stays with me to keep me company and bring me a drink of water now and then. I'm sweating profusely but enjoying the thought of modeling the Kong suit for important visitors. When they arrive, Chiari makes imperious gestures and says something to Paolo in Italian. It seems he asks Paolo to put the mask on me; however, after some discussion, it is agreed that Paolo can carry it along in his hands.

Mr De Laurentiis is impeccably dressed in a gray suit – the picture of elegance. His steel gray hair and chiseled features give him an air of absolute authority. Beside him stands a tallish man with a relatively youthful face (Robert Evans?) and a petite blond woman who I take to be his wife or some other person of intimate acquaintance. I've heard that Mr De Laurentiis inspires such awe among the Italians that whenever they hear he's coming, they go into a frenzy of cleaning up the shop, putting flowers in vases, and spraying the air with cologne. The power of the man, however, inspires frivolous impulses in me, and I feel a tingly sensation in my toes as I approach the group.

I'm completely encased inside the Kong suit except for my blond hair and blackened eyes, giving my face a raccoon-like appearance. Once again, the urge to Charleston comes over me, and I go into a modified version of my dance, shuffling my gorilla feet across the floor. The visitors smile and chuckle, but Mr De Laurentiis is clearly not amused. Chiari seems about to have a heart attack: all I need now are the cap and bells to complete the picture. The little blond woman giggles and reaches out to touch the breasts of the gorilla. I consider telling her about the condoms but think better of it. Mr De Laurentiis is giving me a very stern look, so I retreat to an inconspicuous corner, giving him the floor. Seizing the moment, he takes the Kong mask from Paolo and holds it proudly aloft to the complimentary clucking sounds of his visitors.

"What's it made of?" asks the blond woman.

"It's a ver-ry special-a material," says Mr De Laurentiis.

"It's-a rubber," says Paolo.

Monday April 26

"Metiamo la testa!"

"Where's the tube, T-U-B-E, tube?"

"Ah – il tubo de respiratzione."

"For God's sake, doesn't anybody speak English around here?"

"Now jussa relax, Rick."

"Que tal con los manos, Isidoro?" says Rafael. "Es muy importante!"

"Raphael, what's happening over there?" barks Mr Guillermin. "Can't you get those Italians moving? Hey! – Hey! Ici, boys, ici! Yes, over here you bloody fellows. Dépêchez vous! C'est impossible de travailler sans le gorilla. Nous vous attendions par deux heures!"

"Right away, Mr Guillermin – Madre de Dios! Paolo, tell Isidoro we'll all be castrated – si, castrato – if we're not on the set in five minutes!"

"You jussa tell Missa Guillyman to keep-a his pants on."

Today, the first day of principal shooting with Kong and the miniature sets, the sound stage becomes a scene of mass confusion. Just like the Biblical story of the Tower of Babel, some agent of the Almighty seems to have descended on the multitude, causing them to speak in different languages, unintelligible to one another.

Guillermin speaks French, Paolo and Isidoro speak Italian, and Raphael speaks Spanish. Attempts are constantly being made to bridge the language barriers, but the results don't seem too promising. A few days ago, Bill Kronik was conducting a test on Stage 15, and he tried to pick up a few Italian words in the process. He guessed from a conversation of the Italians that 'bocca' meant mouth. So when he wants Kong's mask to change expression to utter a roar, he keeps shouting 'bocca, bocca!' To Isidoro and the other Italians, however, Bill Kronick is being about as specific as if he were shouting 'foot, foot!' if he wants Kong to move.

"Bocca, bocca!" Kronick shouts. "Is anybody back there listening to me? I feel like I'm talking to myself!"

"Che cazzo li volio?" asks Isidoro.

"Paolo," I say, "what does 'cazzo' mean?"

"Heh-heh." Paolo chuckles, "It means-a 'peanuts'."

"Peanuts?"

"Yeah, like 'Testa di Cazzo', means-a, 'peanuts head'."

"Peanuts? I still don't understand."

"Ah," Paolo said, lowering his voice and pointing to the fly of his trousers, "You know, you know – all-a de men got a peanuts."

Tuesday April 27

Today, the company assembles on Stage 25, the miniature Great Wall set. It's amazing to see how this wall duplicates the one on the back lot. If fact, it's hard to tell which is a copy of which. The miniature wall isn't being used, however, since Guillermin is still making tests on the Kong suit and facial expressions against a black backdrop, off to one side of the sound stage.

I'm required to pose as Rick's stand-in for lighting set-ups, and my self-esteem suffers as a result. It's becoming more and more difficult for me to accept my secondary role, though I'm being well paid. What's more, I'm beginning to feel that Rick's early solicitousness of me has come to an end. After several hours in the suit and mask, he is clearly worn out, and the scleral contacts are giving him problems with his eyes. I'll gladly take a turn in the suit if he wants a rest, but he and Guillermin have begun working together, and he seems determined to carry on. He has a special, air-conditioned dressing room now, and we don't seem to have much to say to each other any more.

I've been given one of the portable, knotty-pine dressing rooms of my own, but it's also being used by the ADs, the Italians, and everyone else. Even the doughnut war between the grips and the maintenance men invades the sanctity of my temporary abode.

This morning when I report for work, one of the grips asks me if he can stash the sack of morning doughnuts in my closet in order to keep them away from the maintenance men who hover around the coffee wagon in the hope of scoring the sweets before anybody else can get to them. Not wishing to offend, since my personal worth in the company is so tenuous, I agree. I realize the foolishness of my decision when, at mid-morning, a burly, bald-headed maintenance man bursts into the dressing room without knocking.

"You got dem doughnuts, doncha!"

"Now, look," I reply.

The intruder pushes past me and starts opening closet doors and looking through drawers, as if I'm not even there. Fortunately, the cache has already been removed by one of the grips. I briefly think the intruder might go berserk if he can't find his crullers, but he finally gives up and stomps out, slamming the door as he goes.

Raphael later twists the doorknob back and forth several times before knocking loudly.

"Will – Will, open up!"

"Who's there?"

"It's Raphael! Why is this door locked?"

"Doughnuts!"

"Doughnuts? Really now, Will. Please come out; your presence is requested on the set."

Wednesday April 28

"If you want to see some shooting out on the wall tonight, I'll leave a pass for you at the gate," Raphael says in a shaky voice as he sits in the dressing room, nursing a black cup of coffee. It's 7.30am and I am wide awake on Stage 25, but Raphael's eyes are bloodshot, and he looks like he's ready to commit murder for a good night's sleep. The entire crew has been working double shifts for the past week, shooting on the sound stage during the day and out on the back-lot at night. Even though May is approaching and the promise of warm days lies ahead, the nights are still chilly and damp. Intermittent rain sometimes sabotages the efforts of the production crew, particularly on the back-lot, and the Director is working his legions to the limit, trying to keep on schedule. Delays in a movie of this magnitude can be financially catastrophic, so John Guillermin is laying siege to the Great Wall on Skull Island every night he can.

The citizens of Culver City are complaining about the native drums going on late into the night, and I'm told that someone, in an effort to calm the troubled waters, has made a sizeable contribution to the local constabulary. In addition, I learn that the term 'Japanese Epic' is taboo for King Kong Productions. There are to be real spectacles in this picture, not cardboard mock-ups of jungles or city skylines. The days when thousands of extras could be kept in tents on the Columbia Ranch for silent sword-and-sandal epics are gone, but that was another era – when Beverly Hills was an orange grove and Sunset Boulevard wasn't even paved in some places. Now the extras are unionized. Film and television production companies still say, "A rock is a rock, a tree is a tree – shoot it in Griffith Park," but now the stakes are much higher.

The night sky over the back-lot is lit up by huge arc lamps mounted on tall wooden towers like beacons, and the smoke from the burning carbon rods rises up into the darkness like the watch fires of an ancient army. Charcoal fires smolder, and an incense-like smell hangs in the air. The 'natives' – actors and dancers – are costumed in a brilliant array of exotic feathers and shells under blankets they keep wrapped around themselves to keep back the cold. All at once, the ADs begin shouting into bull-horns, the blankets are put aside, and the tribe steps forth in all its primal splendor. Guillermin, still looking like a destroyer commander, though wearing a parka and a knit cap with a bright yellow pom-pom on top, rides the camera boom up into the night.

"Is everybody ready? Cameras rolling? ("Speed" – a camera operator calls out as the camera reaches its maximum revolutions) Rayh-t, Action!" booms Guillermin through a bull-horn. Suddenly all the shells, feathers and drums come to life, a gathering of humans, fighting to keep back the gloom of the forest. Hundreds of extras, carrying torches, run up the ramps to the top of the Great Wall. The soundtrack roars over loudspeakers, a mixture of drums, clashing cymbals and voices chanting, "Kong – Kong!" in the cold night air.

"Malem ma Pakeno! Kong wa bisa! Kow bisa para Kong."

The resonant words of Noble Johnson who played the role of the native chief in the original 1933 *King Kong* echo back over forty-three years. The ghosts have returned.

I can feel the earth trembling under my feet; this is it! Here is the feeling of magnificence! It seems as if all my exotic dreams and nightmares come back to me in one, ecstatic instant. Here I am, witnessing part of one of the greatest adventures ever conceived, and it seems so real.

For an instant, I am thrown back into another time, another place where a giant creature moves through a jungle, trampling everything in its path.

Long after the shooting concludes and the actors and dancers return to the scant comfort of their charcoal fires and blankets, the reflective mylar screens shimmer in the light of the arc lamps and seem to cast reflections of flames against the Great Wall.

I walk through the giant gate that has been left ajar as if someone or something has just passed through, and I walk up to the sacrificial altar where Dwan first meets King Kong. I am by myself out there, all the remaining activity taking place on the other side of the wall. I stand between the sacrificial stakes and peer out into the darkness.

"Hey, man, watch out or Kong's gonna get you," cries out a feathered 'native' actor high up on top of the wall.

'That's okay," I shout back. "I *am* Kong!"

Friday April 30

Eureka! I went out to Dr Braff's office in El Monte today and put the scleral contacts on without fainting! I'm as proud as can be, though it takes me at least a half-hour to accomplish the task. I wear them for two hours straight this afternoon, and Rick is obviously impressed. His eyes are still giving him problems and he's talking about consulting another optometrist out in the valley.

When I first put the sclerals on, everything is blurred, but gradually my eyes adjust to the fluid inside the lenses, and I can see almost clearly. I feel a little dizzy at first, but the fishbowl effect is reduced since the lenses have been modified to match my regular eyesight. My peripheral vision is considerably narrower, and the adjustments my eyes are making with the contacts makes me feel as if there are two people inside my head – one who is looking at what I'm seeing, and another who is observing the whole process. When I remove the lenses after wearing them for some time, everything seems blurred, and there are bright, spectral halos around the lights, owing to the saturation of my corneas with the saline lens solution.

The giant creature moves through the jungle, trampling everything in its path

"Roll (Speed) Rayh-t, Action! HUNHH, HUNHH – ROARR! You sniff her, GRMPHH! Sniff again – she screams! ARGHHEROARRR! You turn away."

I notice that both Guillermin and Kronick engage in the most exaggerated face-making and guttural noises whenever they're directing Kong sequences. At one point, Kronick is working with Rick in the suit at the miniature wall, since Guillermin is occupied elsewhere.

"Roll 'em (Speed) Action!" shouts Bill Kronick. "You're angry! HUNNH. You see Wilson! Get that son-of-a bitch!"

All the Kong scenes are being shot MOS – 'Mit Out Sound' (without sound), an old film term used by a German director that has become film jargon, meaning the sound will be added later in post-production. The Italians pull the levers, Kong's face contorts in a silent roar, and to my amazement practically every other face on the set is snarling sympathetically with Kong! Rick does set-up after set-up under Kronick's direction – Kong crashing through the forest, Kong attacking the wall after Prescott and Dwan escape. I'm getting fed up with being the stand-in, holding the bear hide up for lighting and camera adjustments. I look around me at the miniature forest and reflect how different it seems from the 1933 version. Gone are the agonized landscapes reminiscent of Gustave Doré, the jungles seething with life. Visions of that original Skull Island are firmly implanted in the minds of generations.

> *Bottomless vales and boundless floods,*
> *And chasms, and caves, and Titan woods,*
> *With forms that no man can discover*
> *For the tears that drip all over;*
> *Mountains toppling evermore*
> *Into seas without a shore;*
> *Seas that restlessly aspire,*
> *Surging, unto skies of fire ...*

Willis O'Brien might've sought inspiration from Poe's poem *Dreamland* when he conceived the setting for Skull Island in the original *King Kong*, but now, as I look around me, all I can see is a grove of what looks like miniature trees (no doubt to match the natural look of Kauai where all the island location shooting took place). No hanging vines, no weird light penetrating the gloom, no steamy swamps, no bottomless lagoons – our miniature forest reminds me of cow pastures in Northern California's Marin County. I'm tempted to search for miniature cow flops on the ground.

And there are no dinosaurs. The script indicates that Kong fights a giant serpent at one point, but otherwise there is a distinct absence of prehistoric creatures in this version of *King Kong*. Perhaps Mr De Laurentiis feels the dinosaur theme has been overdone. The new story, as told in Lorenzo Semple Jr's screenplay, fleshes out the principal characters and makes Kong even more human-like than the original, but only time will tell if this approach is successful.

Wednesday May 5

This morning at 10.32am David McGiffert – a short, thin, athletic AD – comes to my dressing room and tells me I'll be used in the next production shoot. Needless to say, I am ecstatic! Paolo comes in with the inner suit and congratulates me.

"Okay, Weel, what I tell-a you? Be-leem-o-not (believe me or not), I always know datta one day you be in-a de picture."

David tells me I'll need the 'eyes', so, I immediately set about putting the scleral contacts on. I suppose I'm nervous since this is the first time I'll be in front of the camera for real, and the lenses keep popping out into my hands. I wipe my eyes with tissue after tissue, and the carpet begins to stink because I've spilled lens solution everywhere. Rick comes in and sits on the couch, offering advice and moral support. Every few minutes David checks to see if I am ready, but time after time I drop one of the lenses on the fuzzy carpet and have to start all over.

After repeated attempts I finally succeed, but I've taken forty-five minutes to get the contacts in. I finally step into the inner suit, and it fits me like a glove! Paolo's alterations have done the trick, and without further ado he and Isidoro attach the chest after filling my breast pockets with water-filled condoms. When the full suit has finally been secured, I'm marched out onto the sound stage. A make-up man blackens my eyes, and there are a series of comments from the crew like "Oh yeah" and "So he's finally goin' to work!" The arm extensions are attached to my wrists with gaffers tape while I grope around for the four rings in each arm extension that will give me some control of movement in the gorilla fingers. Finally, I'm completely Kong from the neck down, and I feel so good I begin to dance again in the costume until Bill Kronick, who is directing, asks me not to stir up the dust.

Finally, I'm Kong - from the neck down

"So 'The False Dimitri' is finally getting his chance," says Kronick. "How do you feel?"

"Fine, just fine," I say, grinning from ear to ear. "What do you want me to do?"

"Well, we're doing the sequence just after Kong has chased Dwan and Prescott back to the wall. They've gotten away, and Kong is really pissed off. Kong sees Wilson on top of the wall and thinks it's Prescott. You know, all white men look alike, and you start hitting the wall. You grab for him, but you can't quite reach him. You start pounding along, down the length of the wall towards the gate, and then, well, that's another shot. Okay, try to knock some of these loose pieces of wood off while you're at it, really bash the friggin' thing. We've got to see dust and debris flying, or you're gonna look like some guy in an ape suit, banging on the door of a Samoan outhouse."

The great Kong head with its many expressions is finally lowered over my own head, and the cables are stuffed down the back of the suit, coming out at the ankle. It's very warm in the suit – I'm already sweating buckets – but I love it. I feel strange – wonderful, yet strange. The Kong suit fits so snugly, it feels like a second skin. As I look out through the distortion of the contacts, I see a miniature world spread out before me. I look down at the large, hairy gorilla arm extensions and hands, and a surge of adrenalin goes pulsing through my veins. Something comes over me; I don't feel quite human any more. The voices of the people around me seem far away – all I can hear is the sound of my breathing in the mask.

Then Kronick calls out, "Awright, quiet! Roll cameras (Speed), Action! You see Wilson. ARGHHHH! You're gonna tear that son-of-a-bitch apart! ROARRRR! Missed him, shit! Now start banging the wall!"

Between takes for the Great Wall scene

After I begin the movement, Kronick's voice seems to fade away till all I can hear is my own, low-throated growls and breathing inside the mask. Each 'take' is sheer heaven and I wait anxiously, anticipating the next.

"Cut!" yells Bill Kronick. "Okay, let's wrap it up."

Too soon – too soon! I look above me through the scleral contacts and imagine I see brilliant colors – maybe the spectral halos around the lights.

"That was fine, Will," says Kronick. "This suit looks much better on you. Wait a minute."

He turns to the AD and says, "David, come over here will you? Is it only my way of seeing it, or is there some gap – the mask doesn't seem flush with Will's face." Turning to the cameraman, Kronick asks, "Did you notice that on camera, Hal?"

"Not much, but there is a definite space between his face and the mask – it'll most likely show up in close-ups."

"Have any of the masks been made to fit you?" Kronick asks me.

"No," I say.

"David, get hold of Carlo Rambaldi and find out if any of the masks are being made specifically for Will."

Isidoro and Paolo unhook the mask and gently lift it off my head. The black make-up around my eyes is streaming down my face in streaks and my hair is matted against my head, but I feel tremendous.

"Good boy, Weel," Paolo says. "What I tell you? Now-a you King Kong, too."

I am ushered across the sound stage into Rick's air-conditioned dressing room where the carpet smells of spilled lens solution. Rick pokes his head in, smiles and says, "Hey, what are you guys doing in my dressing room?"

Paolo starts taking off the bear fur with great efficiency. Both he and Isidoro fumble in the fur for the clasps, remove the arm extensions taped to my wrists, and start unhooking the chest, taking great care to remove the water-filled condoms and collect them in a cardboard bucket. In what seems no time at all, I am out of the suit, standing in the middle of the dressing room in my sweat-soaked T-shirt and briefs.

"Thank you Paolo, thank you Isidoro. Grazie al tutti," I venture to say.

"Grazie al cazz!" says Isidoro and smiles. The two of them then collect the sweaty Kong suit, leaving me alone in the dressing room to take out my contacts. Here I finally am, in a 'star' dressing room at last, even though I'm sharing it with Rick. Who cares if the carpet stinks? I can't believe what I look like in the mirror, but after drying myself off with a towel I've been carrying in my knapsack since February, I sit down at the make-up table and begin to remove the scleral contacts. I clean them and put them neatly away. My eyes are red and bloodshot, and I'm seeing halos around the lights.

After cleaning off the black make-up from my eyes and putting on clean underwear, I dress in my green jogging suit. I pick up a Kong arm extension that has been overlooked and take it over to the dressing room reserved for the Kong suits and other accessories. Paolo and Isidoro are gone, and I take a few minutes to look over the amazing collection of suits, masks, feet and hands, plus levers to move the mask's facial expressions. Then I notice a tiny rubber doll in one of the buckets in the room. I take a look at it and discover that it bears a striking resemblance to Jessica Lange. I pick it up in my hand and marvel how even the tiny face looks very much like the leading lady.

The doll is nude and anatomically correct, so of course I can't help wondering how physically close it is to the original. I quickly put it back in the bucket and leave the dressing room.

Wednesday May 19

"I gotta joosta de ting to make-a you head fit," Paolo remarks as I come in to work.

"What are you talking about, Paolo?"

"Rambaldi is-a no gonna make a mask joosta for you. He always say he too busy, but I got joosta de ting," he said as he held up a piece of foam rubber sewn into a black cloth. "We joosta haf to put dis ting onna back-a you head befo' we put on-a de mask. Den it fit fine."

"That's a great idea, Paolo," I say. "Hey it looks like a foam rubber yarmulke. I'll be a kosher Kong!"

"A what?"

"A Jewish gorilla!"

"Why you always talk-a funny, Weel? Plees, lessa try it on under de mask-a."

Paolo saves me from the bench once again – and none too soon! I'm scheduled to break through the 'giant gate' of the Great Wall miniature and fall into a pit saturated with 'chloroform' or some other knock-out gas. The miniature pit is about eight feet long by four feet wide and it's about three feet deep. Despite the fact that there are rubber gym mats in the bottom, I'm a little nervous. Special effects men are filling it with synthetic fog and dry ice. Once I've fallen in, I don't know how I'll be able to breathe.

Thankfully, I'm not required to wear the lenses and only need to have my face blackened. After I'm suited up, I feel such a surge of energy that I jog over to the set and jump up on a three-foot high platform in one leap.

"Save it, Dimitri, You're gonna need that energy," Kronick says to me as he smiles over a cup of coffee.

"Okay, boss," I say. "Just let me at it."

"Here's the pitch," Kronick says. "You saw how Rick was pounding the door a few days ago? Well, we only have a few gates left, so you've got to do it right in one or two takes. We'll be shooting you in slow motion, seventy-two frames per second, from the other side of the wall. Now I want you to lean heavily on the gate, three or four times, then start pounding it with your gorilla glove. At one point, you'll knock a hole through it – you'll see the mark on the other side of the door. Then come blasting through, but make sure you don't go too far or you'll fall right into the pit. After you've broken through, take a moment and give us a roar, looking from side to side. Then all you have to do is fall into the trap."

Grrrroar!

"Is there any particular way you want me to fall?" I ask.

"Well, it's gotta look like you don't see it coming."

"You mean I don't see anything funny about the symmetrically arranged camouflage directly in my path?"

"Hell, no! You're furious! You want to kick ass and take names. You haven't got time to inspect the foliage to see if it's real."

The Kong mask is lowered onto my head and I'm given the plastic breathing tube while final adjustments are being made to the lights. Finally, when the mist on the other side of the wall and the smoke in the pit reach their proper proportions, the breathing tube is taken away and I'm ready to go. I make some last-minute calculations, then I crouch behind the gates, swaying back and forth to pick up steam.

"Cameras rolling? (Speed) Action! Okay, start leaning on the gates – that's it! Now, punch the gate a few times. Awright, put your fist through it – no, no, no – CUT!"

I overestimate the strength of the balsa-wood gate and put my fist completely through, all the way up to my Kong shoulder. We soon set up for another try and I'm once again building up steam behind the gates.

"Will, can you hear me?" says Kronick. "Okay, just tap it this time, *tap it!* Don't let your fist go all the way through. Cameras rolling? (Speed) Action!"

I start leaning against the gates, then take swats at it. I put the gorilla fist slightly through the wood and then hear Kronick yelling at me from the other side of the wall.

"That's it – that's it! Now come through the door, ARGHHHH!"

I take one step backwards, aiming my shoulder at the center of the two doors, then come crashing through, (CAAA-RUNCH!). Pieces of balsa-wood fly left and right. I stand poised on the edge of the camouflaged pit in front of me, raise my Kong arms and growl (GRRRROAR!). Then, looking from side to side, I turn slightly to my left as if my gorilla foot has caught on something. Executing a half-twist of gargantuan grace, I topple into the pit on my back, crashing through the miniature camouflage as if it were made of matchsticks, (BA-WOMPF!). All of a sudden there is a thick, white vapor all around me, the smell from the oil of the fog machines, and the odor of dry ice. I gag and try not to breathe.

"Awright, Will, move around in there – let's see some activity!"

Only a few seconds elapse before Kronick finally yells, "Cut!" but it seems much longer. Then I'm being helped out of the pit: to my amazement, the crew is applauding! It makes me feel very good, as if I'm now a bona fide King Kong.

"That was great, Will," Kronick says, "but I'd like to try it once more. Everything went fine – the pounding, coming through the door, the fall – now, the fall was so graceful. Could you try another variation with a little less 'ballet'?"

"Sure," I say, knowing exactly what I'll do. Everything goes as before, only this time, after crashing through the miniature gates, looking from side to side and roaring, I start moving forward like a forty-foot tall express train, putting my gorilla foot right through the camouflage and falling face-down with a crash. The fumes immediately begin to choke me, I wait a few seconds, and then start to raise myself up on one arm to get out of the pit. At that instant I realize the Director hasn't said, "Cut," the cameras are still rolling, and I think I've ruined the shot.

Falling into the pit with less 'ballet'

"Shit!" I say in frustration, smashing my gorilla arm down on the gym mats and the camouflage debris.

"Cut," yells Kronick.

As I'm being helped out of the pit, he comes over to me and says, "That last fall was great. It looked like Kong realized he couldn't beat the gas, and he went down fighting with one last futile gesture."

"Oh?" I say as I'm being led away by Paolo and Isidoro. The shot subsequently becomes part of the movie.

Saturday May 22

"Hey," Rick says. "Do you know what somebody on Stage 25 said yesterday?"

"No – what?"

"One of the grips came up to me and told me to start looking for a new job. He said, 'We've got us a new gorilla!'"

"Aw, forget it."

We both laugh, but some tension had been mounting in the last two days, since my miniature wall break-through. A motion picture company is like a small town, complete with gossip and competition, and my 'stock' had gone up with the rest of the company, especially the Second Unit. Now people say 'hello' to me when I come in to work. Rick is still doing the 'gorilla's share' of the Kong shooting, but my value as a performer is clearly on the rise. Some of the crew ask me if I'm Rick's stunt double. In addition, my new status results in some changes. For instance, I tell Nate Haggard that I don't think I should be doing any more stand-in work.

"Look, Nate, I was hired as an actor," I say.

"Fine, all you had to do was let me know," he says.

"You mean you would've kept using me as a stand-in, in addition to my other work, if I'd never brought it up?"

"Of course," says Nate with a grin.

Kong is only a role to be played as written, but there are no clear directions and at least two distinct approaches – mine and Rick's. Bill Kronick tells me we are virtually interchangeable, but I know there is a difference. Phil Tucker in editing runs some of my 'dailies', or film sequences in the projection room, along with some of Rick's. We look the same – same gorilla body, same gorilla face, same gorilla expressions, but the movements are different. Rick tends to move his Kong shoulders up and down, first one and then the other, as he walks, swaying from side to side. He keeps his Kong arms bent with his gorilla hands hanging down in front. I, on the other hand, try to match Kong's size, weight and power with his environment. The original Kong, animated through stop-motion photography, had fluidity to his movements that translate on screen as immense size, weight and power. Kong is neither human nor animal, but a combination of both.

We are both trying to keep Kong from looking mechanical or artificial, like a man in an ape suit. Bill Kronick tells me that the real artistry in the film is done by the Director and the Cinematographer. But something or someone has to animate the imaginary creature; Rick and I are more than bodies inside a gorilla suit. There is a living presence inside that gargantuan creature, a mind and soul that completes the process. In some ways, Rick and I are like brothers who share a common, unique experience, a film persona that few, if any, will ever know.

CALIBAN: ... I am all the subjects that you have,
           which first was mine own king.

Tuesday May 25

One of my favorite sequences in Lorenzo Semple Jr's script involves Kong being transported to New York in a supertanker:

> 260A INT. LARGE TANK – DAY (STUDIO) – AN ENORMOUS DARK CAVERN OF STEEL – with a mix of SOUNDS: water rushing along hull plates, throb of ship's engines, roaring air blowers. This is one of the supertanker's oil storage tanks, big enough to hold Notre Dame Cathedral. It is empty and scoured out.
>
> 260B ANOTHER ANGLE – Way up high is an open grillwork through which you see blue sky. MOVE DOWN off that. Down and down, following a slanted beam of sunlight. Suddenly <u>Kong's eyes</u> JUMP INTO SHOT. He is a great dark shape lying on his back on the vibrating floor plates, eyes fixed on that patch of blue sky way up there.

The whole thing is a great, melodramatic piece of exposition intended to develop the relationship between the woman and the great ape. They're taking him away from his island home and he's tortured by his confinement and his attachment to the diminutive Dwan. In the movie, Dwan falls into the cargo hold while trying to communicate with Kong, but he catches her. I watch part of this sequence being shot on the sound stage with Jessica Lange's stunt double, falling from the top of a full size, four-storey mock-up of the hold interior, into an air bag. It's a breathtaking stunt, and everyone gives her a well-deserved round of applause when she emerges from the air bag.

Rick has already begun to work on the miniature tanker set, while I am still busy falling into the pit, but oh how I want to do some of the shooting in the tanker sequence! The miniature tanker set on Stage 15 is a rectangular structure about ten feet by ten feet and fifteen feet high. The walls are made out of sheets of soft metal mounted on a wood frame so that they'll dent easily when Kong pounds on them in his rage.

Tuesday June 1

I'm beginning to think I'll never get a shot at the tanker sequence when David tells me to 'suit up' for Mr Guillermin at 4.30pm. I'm thrilled to know I'll be working with the First Unit at last. After I've had my face blackened and put on the contacts, Paolo helps me into the Kong suit. David

Jessica Lange's stunt-double falls four storeys down into the ship's hold

peeks in and says they're ready for me on the set, and Paolo lowers the Kong head, attaching it firmly to the suit. As I approach the tanker set, Mr Guillermin turns around and speaks.

"Rayh-t! Now who do we have in the suit – Will, is it? Jolly good."

He then turns to Richard Kline and says, "Now, Dick, what do you think of Will's suit?"

"Well, John, it looks darker than Rick's," Kline says.

"Perhaps that's because we kept painting Rick's with that brown 'Streak-n-Tip'," replies Guillermin.

"And the shoulders look a little too padded on Will."

"Ra-ther. Makes him look like Joanie Crawford, doesn't it?"

Regardless of the critical remarks, they decide to go ahead with the shoot.

"Rayh-t. Now, Will, here's what we'd like you to do. We've been working on a shot where Kong sees Dwan high above him on the grille. He makes one great, whacking leap at her but can't quite make it, so he falls back down into the hold. We've been shooting Rick going up, and now we'll be shooting you, coming down."

All my romantic daydreams about playing the tortured beast are torn apart, like a rip in some fat clown's pants. There'll be no suffering, skyward looks for me, no smashing the walls in my anger and pain. It's only Rick going up – and me coming down.

"Now is it possible for you to give us a roar when you land?" asks Guillermin.

I nod, "Yes."

"Fine, I knew we could depend on you."

Dick Kline is crouched in one corner of the set, bending over the camera on the floor that is shooting up at me as I fall. On the count of three I'm supposed to jump backwards off a sawhorse and land on my feet.

"That's rayh-t, Will, on your feet. We can't have Kong landing on his bum now, can we?" says Guillermin.

Having been a diver on my High School swim team, I merely size up the situation, and, after being helped up onto the sawhorse, I balance on the balls of my feet in the gorilla shoes and wait for the imaginary judge's whistle.

"Cameras rolling? (Speed) Rayh-t – Action!"

I hear the imaginary judge's whistle, jump backwards off the sawhorse, and fall flat on my ass.

"Cut!" yells Mr Guillermin, looking like he has just stepped in something unpleasant.

"Jolly good, Will. Let's have another go at it, shall we?"

I finally manage to achieve the desired effect, but somehow I feel I've failed to impress Mr Guillermin. Maybe I tried too hard.

Monday June 7

More days of just hanging around; I spend this morning sleeping in my dressing room. All this inactivity is getting to me again. David McGiffert drops by around noon and slumps into the red armchair, swinging his legs and his green-and-white Adidas shoes over the arm of the chair. He tells me a strange tale of getting drunk on Friday night and going to Las Vegas.

"And I hate Vegas," he says, "but just thinking about what I've been doing here for the past week was enough to make me wanna go."

Dick Kline and David McGiffert

David's problem is just the opposite of mine; he never has a chance to sit down when he's working. In two days the whole company will be going on location to New York. Rick and I, though, will stay behind. On the one hand, it's not too disappointing to get what amounts to a paid vacation while everybody else is working, but it can become tedious. It seems we exist in a rarified environment of fog machines, dry ice and miniature sets. We inhabit miniature worlds and play with dolls. As my mother likes to say, "You go to school for twenty years to become a gorilla?" When anyone at home asks me if I have nightmares, I say 'no'. My dreams can't keep pace with the bizarre parade of my everyday activities.

Monday July 5

Yesterday, the country celebrated its bicentennial. There were tall sailing ships going up the Hudson River, mammoth parades down Fifth Avenue, and the Statue of Liberty blossomed with column after column of colorful fireworks. The First Unit had already returned to Los Angeles, but the Second Unit was still on hand in New York to film some pyrotechnics for Kong's debut.

Supposedly, there have been record crowds turning out to be filmed with Kong's huge carcass at the foot of the World Trade Center. Yes, a full-size Kong had finally been assembled – a complete styrofoam body and horsehair exterior, that is. The forty-foot tall mechanical Kong is still trying to sit up out in the construction shop.

Maybe it'll look better when it gets its horsehair coat

Well, it looks spectacular but it doesn't exactly DO much

Rick is going to be filmed in front of a blue screen, a process whereby a 'plate' of some background – say the New York skyline – can be matted in at a later time. There are delays in setting up the shoot, so Rick and I are ensconced in one of the dressing rooms. Suddenly an aging 'elf" pokes his head in the door and asks Rick if he needs any make-up yet. He looks about fifty-five or sixty, but his short, dyed, blond hair makes such speculation difficult.

"Not yet, Johnny," Rick says, "but why don't you come in and visit for a while?"

The moment I'm introduced to Johnny Truwe, I realize I'm in the presence of one of those magical people who carry history around with them. He has worked at MGM studios for over forty years. He was first noticed by Norma Shearer when he was an errand-boy at the studio in the thirties, then he

Johnny Truwe: a veteran at MGM who knew all the stars

became a make-up assistant and later graduated to make-up man. I saw him briefly before my 'vacation' when he was called in to do special hair work on the Kong suits, where individual hairs were sometimes applied to different parts, particularly the chest. Now, he regales us with stories about the fabulous 'Golden Years' at the studio.

"I mean, stars were simply unapproachable in those days," Johnny says. "And you'd never just walk up to a director and speak to him, you know, like 'Mr So-and So.' Well, after Norma Shearer helped me get started in the make-up department – I was a bus-boy in the commissary before that – but one day I walked right up to her and said, 'Oh, Miss Shearer, I'm sure I'd make a good make-up man if only you'd help me get a start.' And what do you know, soon I was holding a make-up tray for *The Wizard of Oz*, imagine! Now Liza is here doing *New York, New York* – why, it's just like seeing her mother again."

Johnny has an inexhaustible supply of anecdotes about studio stars in the Golden years of moviemaking, including stories about Lionel Barrymore's false eyebrows and Wallace Beery's petty thefts.

"And I have some marvelous souvenirs," Johnny says. "I have the buffalo robe that Robert Taylor died in when he was making *The Last Hunt*."

"You mean Robert Taylor died in a buffalo robe when they were shooting *The Last Hunt*?" I ask.

"No, no, no – in the movie! He died in a buffalo robe in the movie!"

Wednesday July 14

This morning when I arrive at Stage 15, a fat, unshaven technician comes up to me and asks, "Are you one of the guys in the gorilla suit?"

"Yes."

"Then you're gonna need *this*!" he exclaims, pulling out something from behind his back – an enormous styrofoam penis with testicles, at which he roars with laughter. I make a quick getaway to the dressing room.

"I oughta get a kickback for letting you do this scene," Rick tells me as I'm being suited up.

"What are you talking about?" I say. "It's going to be murder on top of that scaffolding."

"So what? I hear, from a very reliable source, that John is going to shoot the scene where Kong takes Dwan's clothes off."

"What?"

In the original *King Kong* there were some famous out-takes that were never part of the final print, where Kong stripped off some of Fay Wray's clothing and then sniffed his fingers. No great scandal – Fay kept her bosom covered – but Kong's finger-sniffing was a bit outrageous for 1933 audiences. In the current script by Lorenzo Semple Jr there is, indeed, a scene where Kong starts to take off Dwan's clothes as he caresses her with his massive fingers. Whether or not the scene is meant for foreign distribution is unclear, but the scene does exist and is going to be shot.

No wonder today Jessica is chain-smoking in the dressing room next-door.

When I'm finally suited up, I'm escorted across the sound stage like a gorilla astronaut being led to the loading ramp for a trip to the moon. I don't need the contacts or any make-up because I will only be the foreground (showing the back of the Kong head mask and my shoulders and upper arms) for a shot involving Dwan and the full-size mechanical arms and hands in front of full-scale, styrofoam cliffs. The wooden apple boxes where I'm to

The giant mechanical hands

stand are at the top of a shaky scaffolding about twenty-five feet high. Since there is no lift, I'm forced to climb the scaffolding in costume. That must be quite a sight. Fortunately, I'm wearing a glove variation of the gorilla hands, which make Kong's arms look ridiculously short but fit over my own fingers.

With each grasp of my rubber Kong fingers, combined with the weight of the costume, the scaffolding sways back and forth. I catch a glimpse of Isidoro, below my furry legs, climbing up right behind me. His knuckles whiten as he grips each rung of the scaffolding, and beads of sweat are forming on his forehead.

"Porca la miseria! Oh Mamma mia – che cazzo!" Isidoro moans.

When I finally reach the top, I find the platform to be about five feet square with a flimsy rail on two sides. The front and right-hand side of the platform are left open, offering easy access to the concrete floor below.

The camera swings up on a boom crane behind the scaffolding with the Director and Cameraman safely strapped into their seats, while the rest of us hold on to each other for dear life. Isidoro is breathing heavily and groaning; I manage to communicate with him in French and discover he is susceptible to vertigo. Using an actor's trick I'd learned to fight dizziness, I tell him to stretch his arm toward the top of the sound stage and look at his hand. Mr Guillermin, however, is unhappy with the particular Kong head that has been brought up, so poor Isidoro has to go down and climb up the scaffolding several times before the Director is satisfied.

Jessica is wandering around the sound stage floor in her bathrobe, which modestly covers her pagan dress and keeps her warm. Inside the gorilla suit I have no trouble keeping warm – in fact I'm sweating profusely. Usually a fan is provided on the set to give Rick or me some measure of comfort, but there is no place for a fan on top of the scaffolding, and I am now having difficulty seeing through the sweat that's pouring into my eyes.

"Rayh-t," says John Guillermin. "Now, Will, if you'll just stand on your mark on top of those apple boxes – good. Now hold your arms out to the side 'cause we have to match them with the two big mechanicals down below. That's it! And could you give us a little movement in the neck and shoulders when we're shooting? Splendid."

Shooting begins, and I pray for it to be over and done with in the shortest possible time frame, but Mr Guillermin isn't satisfied with the movement of the mechanical arms. I bite clear through the plastic breathing tube in my frustration.

"What is the problem, Eddie?" Mr Guillermin calls out through his bullhorn. "We rehearsed the fucking arms this morning – son-of-a-bitch! Why can't we just get on with it?"

Finally the mechanical arms respond to the Director's satisfaction, Jessica takes off her bathrobe and climbs up into the gorilla hand in her native dress, a variation on a grass skirt with shells and feathers, and some fabric covering her chest. She seems uncomfortable sitting in the Kong hand, and, after several takes, John Guillermin speaks to her in French. Their conversation goes something like this:

"Really, my dear, you can't keep pulling your grass skirt over your knees as if you're at a cocktail party."

"That's easy for you to say. You're up there in that camera boom while I'm down here being stared at by these guys, waiting to see my clothes come off!"

Needless to say, the set is eventually cleared of all non-essential personnel, including me and Isidoro, and the filming resumes.

Monday July 19

The First Unit starts out on Stage 27 this morning, then moves to the crater set on Stage 15 to shoot some plates of the giant snake. Yes, high in the craggy, volcanic lair of Kong, a giant reptile menaces the tiny Dwan, and the serpent's great fight-to-the-finish with Kong becomes the picture's only Clash of the Monsters.

Kong approaches his lair

The set is truly fantastic – a miniature Wagnerian dream of smoldering volcanoes, craggy peaks, vertical cliffs, and mist. The long rubber snake, however, is laughable. How in the world can a film budgeted in millions of dollars go in for a rubber reptile? The usual practice is to glue scales or horns on lizards or baby alligators, make them fight, and shoot the action in slow motion – but this won't work, because Kong has to fight this fellow monster. I'm told that a real reptile was considered – some sort of boa – but a twenty-foot long snake, though it might 'read' well on camera, is about as animated as a steaming mound of manure. Not to mention potential injury to the actor

I spend the day wrestling what feels like a giant string of pasta

inside the Kong suit. So what does Rambaldi come up with? A twenty-foot-long piece of rubber, moving along a track in the moss like a toy train. And the head? Right off a cartoonist's sketch-pad: plastic eyeballs mounted in what can be described best in Yiddish as a *'farshtinkener'* (crappy) head with a mouth that opens and closes like the lid of a cigar box, fake curvy teeth, and a mechanical tongue that darts in and out of its hole in the snake's mouth like some bizarre sexual device.

Friday July 30

"Hey, Dimitri!" Kronick calls out to me on the sound stage. "It looks like you're gonna do the snake fight!"

"Are you sure?"

"All I know is that you're scheduled for the main event."

"Is there some way we can rehearse?"

I can't believe my good fortune at being able to do such a dramatic scene: the snake fight is definitely a big action sequence in the film, and I realize that I'll have to work very hard to make it believable. Camera focus obviously can't stay on the snake for very long, or the fight will become hilarious. Fortunately, another wrap-around version of the snake is made for the struggle, but even the graceful convolutions in its rubbery hide are inclined to wrinkle in the clench. Lying by itself on the floor, the snake looks like an enormous pile of yellowish-brown excrement – with teeth.

In doing tests with the snake, running on its track in the moss, Bill Kronick decides it's too fake, so another plan is devised. They'll only shoot a small part of the snake, moving along the track; then they'll cut to it being moved by technicians who will be holding invisible wires off-camera. We rehearse with me in my regular clothing, rolling around with the wrap-around version of the snake, squeezing its neck with my fingers that make its mouth open and close. I'm told, for the finish, I'm supposed to pull the jaws of the rubber snake apart and all sorts of red goo will come out of the mouth. At the end of the day, my hair and clothing are full of fake green moss, and I feel like I've been wrestling a giant string of pasta.

Monday August 2

As I walk onto the crater set this morning, I feel I'm truly King Kong at last. I remember having seen this set when it was nothing more than an irregular set of wooden frames, black plastic drop-cloths and sandy-colored styrofoam. Over a period of months, I've watched it come into being, first as a skeleton of a lost world, taking on a shape and character that gradually becomes unique even to the naked eye. Now a complete world spreads out before me. The mottled grays, greens, blues and browns of the artificial volcanoes blend with the soft olive shades of the miniature foliage to give the impression of some inaccessible terrain, high above the clouds. The large crater seems like a rich, verdant plateau in the sky, and a thin ground fog hovers over what appears to be centuries-old moss and ferns. In spite of all the bustle of the crew, the lights and the special effects, I have a hard time concentrating on what I'm going to do. I'm definitely under the spell of the place, regardless of its artificiality. To me, this set seems worthy of the original Skull Island, a place where no-one has ever been before but which we all intuitively recognize. To one side of the large crater there is a smaller one from whose apertures steam and gas rise upwards like the exhalations of a sleeping giant. Surrounding the set on three sides, a huge cyclorama carries the provocative landscape into farther, receding vistas, beckoning the eye to follow, as in the mysterious, vanishing perspectives in Chinese paintings.

As the Kong mask is lowered over my head, and the cables are adjusted down the back of the suit, I have an expansive feeling that somehow I'm being transformed into a living presence of the myth. We work all day, take after magnificent take, me using the breathing tube in between, but also reveling in the sound of my own breath in the mask as I fight the giant snake. Finally, I tear its jaws apart and its artificial innards pop out. Next we shoot a sequence where I toss its lifeless body to the ground. I want very much to pound my Kong breast and roar after killing the snake, but Bill Kronick says 'no'. For some reason, that's not part of the plan.

Finally, as Paolo and Isidoro get me out of the suit, and I remove the scleral contacts, I see rainbow-colored halos around every light. I'm exhausted but elated. We finish around 7pm and when I go out to my car, I notice a brilliant multicolored halo around the full moon overhead.

An inaccessible terrain, high above the clouds ...

Friday August 6

After my debut in the snake fight, I feel I've achieved more legitimacy in the role of King Kong – more than just 'Rick going up, and me coming down' in the tanker sequence or being the foreground for the Kong-Dwan scene. My work takes a new turn this afternoon, however, when I'm connected to two blue wires attached to a 'flying harness' under the Kong suit and lifted twenty or thirty feet off the sound stage floor in front of a large blue-screen. The camera is a considerable distance away, and Dick Kline is shooting Kong's fall from the World Trade Center, using a zoom lens to create the illusion of Kong falling from far away and coming rapidly closer. I have to keep changing position on the wires because the flying harness is uncomfortable – on my back, upside down, right side up.

"Rayh-t," Mr Guillermin says, "Now Will, what we'd like you to do is sort of a slow roll – yeah, that's it. Let's try a forward roll onto your back. Cameras rolling? (Speed) Rayh-t, Action!"

Suddenly I hear a clatter and a sickening thump followed by a groan somewhere nearby. I strain my position on the wires to see what has happened. An electrician has missed his handhold on one of the wooden light-towers and has fallen about ten feet onto the concrete floor. Everybody seems to rush toward the accident. The whole sound stage is a mass of confusion; an ambulance is called and meanwhile I'm left hanging from the wires, high up in the air. I've been forgotten in the crisis over the electrician, and by the time the ambulance arrives and departs I've been suspended in the flying harness for what seems like an hour. All my shouts and movements from inside the Kong suit go unheard and unnoticed.

Finally, as I hang upside-down, Dave McGiffert approaches me below on the sound stage and asks, "How ya doin'?" Mercifully, I'm then lowered down. As it turns out, the electrician has sustained only minor injuries.

Wednesday August 18

FREE SHOW

DEAR KING KONG:

YES, I WANT TO APPEAR WITH YOU, JEFF BRIDGES, CHARLES GRODIN AND JESSICA LANGE IN PERSON, AS WELL AS 2,999 OTHER CALIFORNIANS IN A PHOTOGRAPHIC SALUTE TO YOU ON AUGUST 11, 13, 18, 20, 1976 STARTING AT 8:00 PM. I AM ENCLOSING A SELF-ADDRESSED STAMPED ENVELOPE TO BE WITH YOU. SEE YOU THEN!

....

....

Admittance to this event gives King Kong Productions, Ltd. and/or its successors the right to photograph me and use my likeness and/or image for sequences in "King Kong."

Los Angeles Times

The second half of Jack Grossberg's announcement is certainly more grammatical than the first; nonetheless, thousands of Kong fans mail in the ad for tickets. Mr De Laurentiis obviously thinks it unnecessary to inform the public that this event will be the one and only appearance of the forty-foot tall mechanical Kong that he has been touting since January.

Originally Kong's New York debut was to be filmed in Shea Stadium, but a skyrocketing budget made it necessary to re-vamp the native wall on the back lot with the appearance of a fictitious corporate spectacle held by PETROX, the oil company in the film that financed the original expedition, and recruit the crowd from the local population. Gone are the hanging vines, the plastic orchids and the interwoven timbers. The wall's primitive exterior has been stripped away and replaced with a shiny, metallic replica of the same wall. Red-white-and-blue bunting is now draped across the top of the wall. The smoke-pots, watch fires and bubbling oil pits have all been cleared away, and now the back lot looks like a High School football field on Saturday night as people began to fill the bleachers.

Behind a silver metallic copy of the sacrificial altar, complete with the same garlands and flowers sprayed with silver paint, stands the mechanical colossus, an impressive sight. The face of the large mechanical Kong bears only a faint resemblance to the masks created for the Kong suits, but perhaps there is a greater sadness in the mechanical eyes, well-suited for the beast enslaved by avaricious promoters and gawking spectators. There have been the usual problems with the weight of the massive machinery. On opening night Kong's belly collapsed, leaving his mighty chin to sag against his chest, but gradually the problems with the machinery were solved, and now it towers with regal splendor, supported by a thick metal column shoved up its rear and a large metal crown placed on its head in mockery of the great beast. The mechanical Kong is heavy, so it is confined to incredibly slow movements of its limbs and face.

... and it weighs a ton

I sit down in a folding canvas chair with Charles Grodin's name on it, hoping he won't mind, and settle back against the bleachers to take in the scene around me. Many of the union extras are filling the bleachers to my right, and a continual crowd of local ticket-holders flows past me.

A Mexican-American couple lead their grandmother to the bleachers amidst blond surfer-girls, long-haired boys wearing Hawaiian shirts, and folks from as far away as San Bernardino who've come in to be part of the movie. Also in the crowd there appear to be some European types – extremely tanned, expertly coiffed and overly made-up – hoping to catch the camera's eye. I see Federico, wearing a leather jacket and moving around the field. He approaches John Guillermin who is working nearby and begins to speak softly in his ear.

"Nah look, Federico," Guillermin says. "Ah've been working on this bloody film for a year; so don't – just don't start making helpful suggestions at this late date. I simply don't have time to listen ... David! Where is that goddamn bloody beer I asked for over an hour ago?"

Everyone obviously wants to be 'seen' at this function, and many of the California girls seem dressed more for the beach than for the chilly night air on the back-lot – bare legs, bulging breasts and neon eye-liner. At that precise moment I notice Charles Grodin, dressed in what looks like a Woolworth's safari outfit. He's been posing for photos with Jessica Lange on the refurbished altar, but now he's looking for his canvas chair.

"I suppose you're looking for your chair, " I say, standing up.

"Who are you?"

"I'm one of the guys in the Kong suit."

"Oh yeah? That's just fine," says a befuddled Mr Grodin as he sits down in his chair.

I stroll off in the direction of the catering truck and pass the Long Beach High School Band, warming up to play 'That's Entertainment.' I quickly pass beyond the brilliant lights trained on the field and meet Bill Kronick in the shadows. He is dressed in what I imagine a Basque partisan might wear – jeans, beret, and a sweater tied around his neck.

"Well, if it isn't 'The False Dimitri'," he says, smiling over his usual cup of coffee.

"Thanks. Got any plans after this thing's over and done with?"

"Oh, I've got a few projects in mind, but I guess I'll just live off the kindness of others like everybody else in this business. It's all a question of timing and luck," he says.

Back at the wall, the big eyes roll on the giant mechanical Kong, the big jaw laboriously opens, and the audience yells and applauds. John Guillermin swings out over the crowd on the camera boom, the ADs bark through their bull-horns and a large mass of people are mobilized to run, screaming, from the giant gorilla that presumably escapes but is, in fact, unable to move.

"Rayh-t," booms Guillermin through a microphone. "Now, will everyone please pay attention: Kong has just escaped and you can't get away from this place fast enough. Now, start to move slowly, then pick up speed ... David, is anybody out there listening to me? I feel like I'm bloody talking to myself – Good evening to you, too, dear. Yes, that's right, I'm the director. All right, Eddie, start the arms moving, now the face. Cameras rolling (Speed), Rayh-t, Action! More of the face, Eddie! Here he comes, folks – he's broken loose ... Cut! Cut! ... Rayh-t, David – let's set it up again ... Can everyone out there hear me? (Roar from the crowd) Good! We're going to do the same shot again, folks, and, please, don't start laughing as you're running away from Kong!"

By 11.30pm the circus is almost over. Jessica Lange and the giant mechanical gorilla can only hold the attention of the crowd for so long – especially when the people in the bleachers have to act out their excitement, over and over. Between set-ups Bob Hastings, a tuxedoed television personality, acts as Master of Ceremonies to keep the crowd's attention with a running monologue about the accomplishments of Dino De Laurentiis, his 'stars', and the magic of Hollywood, but even Mr Hastings gradually gets tired of his own talk, and the carnation in his lapel begins to wilt. A few people get up to go, and soon they are leaving the back lot in droves. I know I'll be involved in shooting on one of the sound stages till early in the morning, so I head over to the catering truck to catch a midnight meal.

For days, Guillermin and First Unit have been working with Rick, shooting sequences of Kong's rampage after escaping from the stadium. There is a scene of Kong attacking the elevated subway train – it has taken weeks to build the track of the 'EL' going through Queens with miniature buildings on either side. This is a very complicated scene with cameras shooting from multiple angles. As in the original 1933 film, Kong attacks the subway train, looking for Dwan and tearing it apart in the process.

Then, in our script, Kong wades across the East River to get to Manhattan. Wading across a water structure on the sound stage, the weight of the Kong suit became so heavy that Rick had to be helped by a special effects man wearing scuba gear. If Rick fell over in the water he might not have been able to get up by himself, and with the mask on he might not have been able to breathe. Fortunately, there were no accidents, but there were clear safety concerns for the man in the suit.

Next, there were a series of shots with Kong coming out of the water in Manhattan and attacking a Consolidated Edison electrical switching station. I don't know how they accomplished this, but there were several exploding electrical effects as Rick/Kong attacked the wires. The Kong suit was clearly wet, and water conducts electricity, however, the feet and hands on the Kong suit were made of rubber, and, as far as I know, Rick didn't have any accidents. Frankly, I admired his courage in going through all this as filming continues during the day and at night. Fortunately, we're rarely involved in double shifts, and because of my SAG contract, they'd have to pay me overtime.

Just then, a sleek Rolls Royce carrying Mr De Laurentiis and his guests passes by, stirring up a cloud of dust. I take off my cap and make a deep bow in the direction of the red tail-lights as they grow smaller and smaller in the darkness. After all, he's paying me.

Kong crosses the East River and rampages through Manhattan

Saturday August 21

The Empire State Building was the tallest building in the world when it was completed in 1932, one year before the making of the original *King Kong*. It stands to reason that Merian C Cooper's 'Make it Bigger' imagination would not have settled for anything less. In so doing, he and fellow producer Ernest B Shoedsack created an American myth of a giant, savage beast conquered by love for a pretty human female. New York was also part of that myth, representing a monument to American industry and ingenuity, the Empire State Building being a ready-made phallic symbol of American power and presence in the world.

If it were simply a question of having the new King Kong climb the tallest building in the country, why wasn't Chicago's Sears Tower in the running? Clearly, Mr De Laurentiis wants to keep the mythic connection with New York, so the World Trade Center is chosen. The fact that the building consists of two equally imposing towers creates a slight problem that is overcome in Lorenzo Semple Jr's script by drawing a parallel between the jagged peaks of Kong's Skull Island home and the New York skyline:

> 434 KONG'S P.O.V. – which is the tops of a group of midtown skyscrapers in silhouette against the full moon. It is déjà-vu all right – just exactly the profile of those craggy spires around the Pacific island eeyrie [sic] where he carried Dwan.

There is really no need to justify the choice of the World Trade Center for the movie; it's enough for audiences worldwide to see Kong climbing the tallest building in New York, because that's part of the myth. Like the classic human hero-warrior, fighting to the death, Kong seeks the highest possible vantage point for his last stand. High above the glittering lights and human cacophony below him, Kong perches with his miniature treasure, Dwan, in an all-too-human posture of defiance and determination. His enemies will overcome him and he has no route of escape – but they'll have to come at him one at a time.

I have been 'climbing' a miniature of the top floors of the World Trade Center for several days on a sound stage in the original MGM studios in Culver City. The miniature World Trade Center is around thirty to forty feet tall, and I am actually being pulled up the side of the set by a winch attached to a groin harness inside the Kong suit. I have to work very hard to make it look like I'm climbing. It's exhausting and I sweat profusely in the suit. Fortunately, there is now an air-conditioned Winnebago parked just outside the sound stage for Rick and me to rest in between set-ups.

Standing on the top of the World Trade Center miniature, I really do feel like I'm standing at the top of the New York skyline. I have a better sense of Kong's size, relative to his surroundings, than I've had working on any of the other miniature sets. The top of the miniature building is a strange place: isolated in the air, it seems above and beyond our normal plane of perception.

I remember gazing across the New York skyline from the roof of a thirty-storey New York University apartment building on Bleecker Street when I was going to school there in the late 1960s. The World Trade Center was under construction then, but it wasn't even half finished, as I recall. Looking toward the southern end of Manhattan, I felt as if I were gazing across the rooftops of some fantasy world where winged people flew between spires and oddly shaped buildings under an orange-blue sky.

When I arrive at the studio this morning, I'm told to get into the flying harness in preparation for Kong's leap between the twin towers. The top of the southern tower – the last several storeys of it – is mounted on a high scaffold. The leap is to be shot at an upward angle from the floor. I am amazed at how realistic the tiny walkways, antennae and flashing red beacons look on the miniature World Trade Center. The set is being shot against a black background that completely absorbs the light from the smoking arc lamps and other instruments, preventing shadows.

I am completely prepared in the Kong suit with blackened face and the flying harness, standing on top of the miniature building. Two large special-effects men hold on to a stout rope attached to wires that is supposed to give me the 'bum's rush' off the top of the building. Finally, Bill Kronick calls out, "Cameras rolling? (Speed) Action!" and I am pulled off the top of the set, making as much of a leaping motion as I can.

The flying harness cuts into my groin as I swing back and forth above the sound stage. I strain to breathe in the suit and start to see spots before my eyes. Then all at once I'm being lowered toward the miniature tower where Hal, one of the special-effects men, grabs me by my gorilla toes and pulls me back onto the top of the set. This process is repeated for several takes, but finally it's over. When the Kong head and mask is finally removed, Paolo helps me towards the Winnebago parked outside the sound stage. The belt makes walking very difficult and a little painful. Sweat plasters my hair against my forehead, and the blackening around my eyes begins to streak down my face. As we come out of the sound stage on an upper loading dock, I see Katharine Hepburn seated in a canvas chair, reading a book. I'm so surprised and excited to see her, I completely forget how I look. "Miss Hepburn, Miss Hepburn," I call out to her, frantically waving a gorilla paw at her. She looks up from the book she is reading, her eyes open wide, and says, "My Gawd!"

Tuesday August 24

John Guillermin is working with Jeff Bridges on a full-scale section of the World Trade Center. He prepares for a take, saying, "Cameras rolling? (Speed) ... Rayh-t, Action!"

Suddenly Jeff appears as Jack Prescott at a window inside the building.

Guillermin calls out, "You try to see Kong on the top! You hear the flame-throwers! Rayh-t! Now Kong jumps! He lands on the other side! He picks some stuff off the roof and throws it at those rotten bahsteds ... Boom!"

I can hear Jeff yelling behind the window, "Kill the assholes! Kill 'em! Kill 'em! – Yayyyyy!"

From what I've seen from the dailies, Jeff's character, Jack Prescott, is one of the best things in the film – except for Kong, of course. Not only is Jeff a good actor, his character seems to be the only voice of reason in the film – the conscience of the audience. Off camera, he is very personable and happy to talk to me from time to time. In fact, he's one of the nicest people I've met at the studio.

Later that day, I'm suited-up to make Kong's jump between the two towers. Before that, however, flame-throwers are supposed to be fired at Kong, singeing his shoulder. I become very nervous. If, by accident, the Kong suit catches fire, I might be seriously burned before the crew can get me out of the suit. Since I have a Screen Actors Guild contract, I can't be forced to do anything that is potentially dangerous, so I ask to see a demonstration of how the 'burn patch' works before I do the shot. A special-effects man brings me a small patch of fur with the burn device on a piece of wood to show me it is practically harmless. He connects the wires and the entire patch is incinerated. I'm horrified. I finally agree to do the shot with two big special-effects men standing off-camera with large buckets of water to drench me if anything goes wrong.

Wednesday September 15

"These used to be called the 'Selznick Studios' in the old days," says Johnny Truwe as we chat over coffee in the Winnebago. "Clark Gable made *Gone With The Wind* here. His salary was – guess what? – five thousand dollars a week, a lot of money in those days, and taxes were nothing like they are today. And, yes, I was with Elizabeth Taylor for four years – Gene Kelly for five. Elizabeth was a wonderful woman. You might not know it, but she's really an introvert – quiet, you know. But, listen, you can believe me when I tell you that Second Unit is the 'Shit Detail' – 'Shit Detail,' that's what it is. Take that cameraman, for instance – you know very well which one. He's been doing 'Shit Detail' for years. Lord, how quiet he is! He never has any expression, never gets mad. It's not that he's no good, it's just that he never makes waves. He's always the same – consistent, you know."

While I can't agree with Johnny that the Second Unit is the 'Shit Detail' on *King Kong*, I can see his point as far as principal photography is concerned. Nevertheless, the Second Unit has given me the chance not only to play the tallest, darkest leading man in the history of motion pictures, but it has also given me the unique experience of seeing the motion picture industry at work – in all its glory and contradictions – with a classic American story.

I realize that probably no-one will ever know I played the role of King Kong except for a select few, but that doesn't matter. Often Rick expresses his dissatisfaction with the lack of credit he's receiving for his contributions to the film. I feel he's right, and I hope time will correct those discrepancies. King Kong Productions makes no disclosure that the forty-foot tall mechanical Kong has been a failure in the actual movie and that the role of the famous screen monster is played by two men in elaborate gorilla suits.

Rick and I had only one location shoot, at a military base down the coast where full size Huey helicopters strafed Rick in the Kong suit with fifty-caliber machine gun blanks on top of some scaffolding. Things were pretty exciting, watching the helicopters come flying down in formation, blasting away with blanks and feeling the empty shells come down on us in a rain of metal.

On location for the helicopter scene

85

Now, it's all over. Finally the film 'wraps' in September: there's a brief wrap party on one of the sound stages, and those of us still left in the cast and crew finally go our separate ways. I drive off the MGM lot for the last time, pondering one of the most unusual experiences I've ever had. It wasn't fate or destiny that led me to this; it was simply my good fortune. My childhood dreams and fantasies suggested a fascination with gorillas and lost worlds, but I never knew this would lead me to become a member of that select group of movie gorilla-men who had gone before, and I have Rick to thank for that. I don't know where my future adventures will take me, but this is one I will long remember.

Friday December 17

King Kong finally opens to great fanfare, and I can't wait to see the finished product. Like thousands of others, I line up at a movie theatre on Hollywood Boulevard, but with the secret knowledge that I was there for some of the shooting at MGM. Also, I can't wait to see if some of my own work is shown on screen. As the lights go down and John Barry's musical score begins, there isn't a sound in the movie theatre.

The story begins, the music and cinematography are great, and I'm waiting to see how the film brings Lorenzo Semple Jr's script to life. My first impression is that most of the actors and characters are good, except for Charles Grodin's character, Wilson, who seems more like a caricature of the scheming, corporate, Petrox oil man. I can't tell if it's the script, the direction, or the acting, but it seems very campy. The film moves along with the discovery of Jeff Bridge's character, Jack Prescott, but then screeches to a halt with the appearance of Jessica Lange as Dwan. The camera seems to spend a ridiculous amount of time on Dwan's vapid dialogue with some of the ship's crew, including Prescott, but the problem seems to be with the way the part is written.

Consequently, it seems to take the film a long time to catch up with the next part of the story, leading to Skull Island and Kong. The location setting on Kauai is beautiful except for an artificial matte shot of the great wall, but the appearance of the 'natives' brings the film back to life. Not having been on the location shooting, I find that part of the story entertaining, but, of course, I want to see Kong.

The momentum picks up with the abduction of Dwan by the 'natives' and their making an offering of her to the great ape. The suggestion of Kong's first appearance, though, seems to be made by tractors or backhoes, pushing some trees back and forth. Then Kong comes into view, in a close-up of his head and shoulders, moving through the forest, and the effect is spectacular. The Kong suit works beautifully, and the scleral contacts create remarkable depth to Rick's portrayal. In later scenes between Kong and Dwan, however, she comes off sounding shallow and self-centered.

Of course, I'm eager to see myself as Kong, but the scene where Rick/Kong shakes the great log, causing most of his pursuers to fall down into the chasm, is exciting. I saw rehearsals of that being filmed at the studio, along with Prescott's escape, and it works well.

Rick as Kong, about to shake the big log

The chasm

As Kong takes Dwan high up to his crater home, the setting is amazing. Then comes the fight between me and the huge 'snake'. Again, it looks silly, but with clever editing it works as I see myself wrestling the rubber reptile and tearing its jaws apart. The exposed snake innards, however, seem fake. When I see myself discard the lifeless body of the snake, it seems incomplete because I wasn't allowed to pound my chest in triumph.

My next appearance as Kong occurs at the gate of the great wall. At first, I can't tell if it's Rick or me pounding on the wall, but yes, it's definitely me – crashing through the gate and falling into the pit. I know it was filmed in slow motion, but I have to suppress a laugh when I realize I'm saying, "Oh shit!" as I go down.

The rest of the movie, including the tanker sequence and Kong's escape from captivity, moves along well, but the relationship between Dwan and Prescott never seems to come together. Frankly I don't know what he sees in her. The appearance of the full-size mechanical Kong at the stadium is completely unconvincing, but Rick/Kong's escape from his metal cage and subsequent path of destruction in Manhattan, on the other hand, is exciting.

My great moment, about to fall into the pit

Kong climbing up the World Trade Center with Dwan is extremely well done, matching the location shooting with the sequence filmed in the studio. I'm amazed that it looks so convincing. In one shot of my Kong leap from one tower to the other, however, I can see the wires attached to the Kong suit. But maybe that's because I know they're there.

The climatic fight-to-the-finish between Rick/Kong and the Huey gunships works very well, including what appears to be me, in the Kong suit, falling from the twin towers. Rick does a great job in the last moments of Kong's life, but the rest of the ending seems to lack something. Still, as I file out with the rest of the theater crowd, I have to admit it's a good movie and should do well at the box office.

AFTERWORD

February 25, 2014

After nearly forty years, Dino De Laurentiis' production of *King Kong* is still regarded as a major motion picture, though dated by limited technology and parts of Lorenzo Semple Jr's script, which hovered close to his more campy work with the *Batman* TV series and the *Flash Gordon* film (also produced by De Laurentiis).

In the 60s and 70s, 'camp' was used as a means of revitalizing older forms of popular entertainment, but, in my opinion, the film fell short of doing justice to the great American myth of King Kong. Dino De Laurentiis was trying to reinvent the story, relying on the huge mechanical gorilla and on the discovery of his new star, Jessica Lange. The production, however, was hampered by the continual breakdown of the mechanical beast and some embarrassing lines given to Dwan, such as, "You goddamn chauvinist pig ape, what are you waiting for? If you're gonna eat me, EAT ME!" Of course, Jessica Lange's role in *King Kong* wasn't worthy of her true talent – that would emerge later in a very distinguished and celebrated acting career.

If *King Kong* was successful, it was – in my opinion – largely due to Rick Baker's portrayal of Kong in the amazing gorilla suit and mask he helped create. Of course, I like to think I helped to create the role, too. The production elements of the film were very good – cinematography, sound and lighting – as was the excellent musical score by John Barry, but it seems to me that there were obvious contradictions that could have been avoided.

For instance, a breathtaking shot of the cast walking in single file along a path on the island of Kauai slowly pulls back to reveal a magnificent landscape of converging canyons as the characters become smaller and smaller, eventually disappearing into the natural spectacle. However, this is soon followed by the cast, on the same island, coming across a painted matte shot of the Great Wall, an obviously artificial substitute. The Kong masks, although very effective, descend into cartoonish farce when the ape grins: his fangs seem to disappear, to be replaced by what looks like human dentures.

Rick's portrayal of Kong's final moments, as he is attacked by helicopters on top of the World Trade Center, was inspired. All the production elements

133 CONTINUED:

Kong studies this curious noise-making thing briefly at arm's length, then starts bringing it in for a better look. Dwan sees the terrible face coming closer...

134 KONG'S P.O.V. - as he brings her in. The wonderful gleaming whiteness of the girl in middle of field of vision, those concentric halos of astigmatism around her. The little mouth opens in another SCREAM -- but again, distortions from the ape's P.O.V. are always aural as well as visual, so what would be a piercing shriek to your ears is heard as melodious to his.

135 DWAN - hands over eyes as she awaits her final moment. The motion STOPS. She opens her eyes. ANGLE QUICK to the godawful ape face barely three feet away.

136 PULL BACK A LITTLE - No motion. Kong just breathing, staring at her, holding her there like on a platter in front of his horrendous mouth. Suddenly Dwan cannot take this tension. She snaps. She springs up to front of the paw, yelling incoherently and flailing wildly at Kong's face, punching around the nose region with both fists. She pauses and yells hysterically:

> DWAN
> You goddamn chauvinist pig
> ape, what are you waiting for??
> If you're gonna eat me, EAT ME!

No response.

> DWAN
> (continuing)
> Eat me! EAT THE WHOLE THING!!
> CHOKE ON ME!!

She slams him again. The negligible blows seem to fascinate Kong rather than anger him. Dwan winds up for another wallop, suddenly freezes in utter horror at what she has been doing. She shrinks backward, drops to her knees and gasps.

> DWAN
> (continuing)
> I didn't mean that! -- I swear
> I didn't! -- Sometimes I get
> too physical, it's a sign of
> insecurity, you know? Like when
> you knock over trees?
> (MORE)

(CONTINUED)

Some of Dwan's lines in the script were pretty embarrassing came together effectively, and Rick/Kong's reaction to the bullets, his fall, and the close-up of Kong's last moments are still moving to watch. The pathos of this scene, however, is weakened by a quick cut to Dwan, approaching the fallen Kong seconds later (how did she get down from the top of the World Trade Center so quickly?), followed by crowd movements at the World Trade Center Plaza, shot previously, showing them all rushing on cue toward the large, fallen, artificial Kong. Despite these minor errors the fact remains that, for many, this version of *King Kong* is faithful to the original: over the years I've met people who remember the film as a cherished part of their childhood.

The subject of the World Trade Center brings up a more troubling issue. In the 1933 version of *King Kong*, at the height of the Depression, the Empire State Building represented not only America's potential as a world power but also a triumph of US industrial might and productivity. In 1976, the World Trade Center represented the dominance of the US as a world economic power. The subsequent attack on the twin towers on September 11, 2001, was a tragic reminder that the US was no longer safe from war and destruction at home. Seeing Kong's fictional fall from the top of the twin towers in 1976 now seems a troubling precursor of the real onslaught that destroyed them twenty-five years later.

Finally, though, was this *King Kong* faithful to the original *mythic* story? For that matter, what *is* the mythic story of King Kong? Scholars and commentators have tied it to colonialism, slavery, racism and miscegenation, but I think the answer is much simpler. *King Kong* is a story of loss and sacrifice. The loss has multiple dimensions – to begin with, Kong's loss of freedom and the natives' loss of faith in believing that Kong was a god to be worshipped. As Jack Prescott says in the film: "He was the mystery and terror of their lives – the magic ... When we took Kong, we kidnapped their God." Next comes the civilized world's moral loss, in the callous belief that such a powerful natural force was something to be exploited for corporate gain. Again, as Prescott says when asked to join the spectacle of Kong in chains at the stadium: "I was wrong. It's not a farce; it's a tragedy."

It may be argued that Kong's fall to inevitable death is symbolically the modern world's 'sacrifice' to a god of power and money. Kong is killed through abduction from his natural world, the avarice of his captors, and the violence of his resistance to subjugation. His weakness in being attracted to so-called 'beauty' seems like an echo of the masculine cliché that loving or caring for a female is weakening to the male. As Carl Denham says in the original motion picture: "When he met beauty, she got him; he went soft, he forgot his wisdom, and the little guys got him." Kong's love for the tiny white woman is, frankly, as hard to believe now as it was then, but we buy it anyway because movie audiences can't resist a love story, and the relationship between the woman and Kong humanizes the great ape.

Something still seems to be missing from our 1976 version. After Kong has escaped and is on a path of destruction in Manhattan, Dwan motions to a deserted bar and tells Prescott, "Buy me a drink," an odd request that makes her seem oblivious to what's going on all around her. At the end of the film, there is a carnival-like atmosphere with spectators gawking at the dead Kong and a melodramatic shot described in the script as 'Dwan in the TV lights, weeping.' In short, nothing seems to have been learned except that a dead, giant gorilla draws a crowd.

What else is possible? I believe there is a universal aspect to the King Kong story – the struggle between powerful natural forces and the human will to survive. The tone and character of the struggle may vary, depending on the story, but what is learned by the outcome becomes even more important.

Kong is a marvelous, mythic creature who in some ways is similar to a human, yet at the same time, very different. His size and power are far greater, but his capacity for affection and attachment is human-like. Kong is protective of the woman and this is what makes his sacrifice so poignant. Taken from the world he knew, all he has left is the tiny human female, and he dies protecting her. It is a unique, if futile, heroic act on the part of the giant ape that makes human actions, by comparison, appear small and petty.

With the passage of time and more perspective, I find that the story is a striking portrait of not only American culture and society but also popular culture worldwide. Peter Jackson's remake in 2005 benefitted from CGI and motion-capture photography and told the story in a way that spoke to a new generation, reflecting its own time and values. What form it will take in the future remains unclear, but I believe the story of King Kong will continue to inspire audiences for years to come.

www.ingramcontent.com/pod-product-compliance
Lightning Source LLC
LaVergne TN
LVHW061220060426
835508LV00014B/1379